An Exile Revisits Cuba:
A Memoir of Humility

An Exile
Revisits Cuba

A Memoir of Humility

GABRIEL NESS

McFarland & Company, Inc., Publishers
Jefferson, North Carolina

Library of Congress Cataloguing-in-Publication Data

Names: Ness, Gabriel.
Title: An exile revisits Cuba : a memoir of humility / Gabriel Ness.
Description: Jefferson, North Carolina : McFarland & Company, Inc.,
Publishers, 2016. | Includes bibliographical references and index.
Identifiers: LCCN 2015046536 | ISBN 9781476665252
(softcover : acid free paper) ∞
Subjects: LCSH: Ness, Gabriel—Travel—Cuba—Havana. | Cuban
Americans—Biography. | Immigrants—United States—Biography. | Havana
(Cuba)—Description and travel. | Cuban Americans—Costa Rica—Puerto
Jiménez—Biography. | National characteristics, American. | National
characteristics, Cuban. | Political culture—United
States. | Political culture—Cuba.
Classification: LCC E184.C97 N47 2016 | DDC 305.868/7291073—dc23
LC record available at http://lccn.loc.gov/2015046536

British Library cataloguing data are available

ISBN (print) 978-1-4766-6525-2
ISBN (ebook) 978-1-4766-2460-0

Printed in the United States of America

McFarland & Company, Inc., Publishers
Box 611, Jefferson, North Carolina 28640
www.mcfarlandpub.com

In memory of my father, Facundo, a great orator and teacher,
and of my mother, Consuelo, my heroine always.

To my brother, Facundo, Jr., who accompanied me through it all,
and to his wife Ruth and my nieces and nephew
Angela, Isabel, and Miguel
for their love and support.

And to the beautiful people of Cuba.

What is a cynic? A man who knows the price of everything, and the value of nothing.

—Oscar Wilde

TABLE OF CONTENTS

Acknowledgments

I'd like to thank my friend Howard for his incisive revision of my manuscript as well as for his lifelong support of my half-baked dreams of becoming a writer.

I also thank my friends Alex, Emilio, Jackie, Mary, Miguelito, Oliver, Tom and Will for their valuable input and support toward the realization of the manuscript.

Please forgive the omission of your good last names.

As always, it's a question of bondage and freedom.

PREFACE

This memoir of a ten day visit to Havana by an exile evolved into much more than I had anticipated. At first, I had planned to write only about my experiences and observations during the trip I took in the summer of 2012 in order to replace my lost birth certificate, which I needed to apply for residency in Costa Rica, where I now live. As I pressed on, however, it became apparent that to limit the work to just the original intent would have resulted in a shallower, less worthy narrative that did no justice to the cornucopia of philosophical implications that Cuba harbors inside its borders for everything outside of them. Cuba is a contrived, dominated world created by the mind of its dictator, Fidel Castro, who borrowed many of the ideas for its creation from the defunct ideology of the old Soviet Union. As such, it is a misplacement in time, still surviving at the doorstep of its converse, the United States. Because my family and I left Cuba when I was nine years old and I had lived in the U.S. until I was 33, I could not ignore the contrast of the two societies and the ramifications that sprang from the dissimilitude. But I went further still. In the end, I turned my observations on myself, took a good look at what the Cuban-American experience had done to me, and the result was an epiphany.

Telling the truth in this world can still get you in trouble, and that's why I've had to lie. It truly is a shame that you can't tell a story about Cuba without changing the names of the people you talked to or even the places you stayed in for fear of the well-being of those people. As a result, in this story I invented all the names that could be used to trace those who spoke to me against the Revolution and even those who spoke to me in favor, for the latter could be used to discover the former. The characters and their actions, however, are all too real. There is an organization called the *Dirección de Inteligencia* or Intelligence Directorate, also known as the DI or the G2, whose business is to identify and neutralize threats to the Revolution not only in Cuba,

1

but also all over the world. The G2 is not to be taken lightly, for the KGB trained its agents, who became its proxies in Latin America. Throughout the world, they have been and are involved in the support of leftist regimes and the dethronement of rightist as well as democratic ones. Like others of their ilk, their list of activities includes counter-intelligence, assassination, terrorism, revenge and extortion.

In this memoir, I use the real first names of my family members. In the story, my own first name, Gabriel, is fictitious and my family's last name remains a secret. Of course, the name on the cover, Gabriel Ness, is an invention, a pen name—if not, there might be a knock on my door some day that may not be good for my health to answer.

The fact that I've had to resort to this should alert the naïve, leftist reader of the nature of the Cuban Revolution. The sister of a close friend of mine from the East Coast once answered a comment I had made about Cuba's dastardly regime by saying that the Revolution had provided the people of Cuba free education, health care and housing and had nurtured the pride, self-respect and dignity they lacked while they were under the influence of the United States. An eventual goal for this memoir was to establish that while the first part of her statement is generally true, the second is nothing but an illusion perpetuated by the naïve and ideologically compromised left, an illusion that likely contributed to the delay in the demise of the Soviet Union and to the enduring embellishment of the legacy of Fidel Castro.

Putting everything and everyone in a box and labeling it is a human tendency that makes us feel good, diminishes our anxiety, our fear. It gives us a feeling that we're in charge and have the former unknown under control. So please don't assume that the narrative about to unfold is just a Cuban-American's rabid diatribe against the Castro regime. It's far from it. I found many good things in Cuba worthy of note. And in the act of comparison to America, I found much lacking in America. So from the outset I encourage you to avoid putting this work "in a box" and to maintain an open mind until the end.

Another reason I felt compelled to write this memoir was to give a voice to the muzzled souls I encountered in Havana: *Pobrecitos*—the "poor dears"—that touched me like no poor or stricken have ever touched me before. Until the island is finally rid of its dictators, we will not know the extent of their suffering or the crimes unpunished against them. But through this memoir, I opened a sliver that allowed a peek at their misery and I became a mouthpiece to their grief.

Now allow me to explain about the roots of the Revolution, and its latest developments since my trip, so that you may better understand what it was all about and where it might go.

If you had asked a contemporary historian in 1958 what was the most likely country in Latin America to undergo a communist revolution, the last place she would have considered would have been Cuba. Contrary to popular belief that the island was a hellhole of inequality, poverty and social injustice before Fidel Castro's coup d'état in January 1959, Cuba in reality ranked among the most advanced and prosperous countries in Latin America. To be sure, there was a dictatorship and there was much social injustice in 1958 Cuba, but certainly less than in most Latin American countries of that era. Havana was a sophisticated, glittering and vibrant city. The country's economy in the first half of the 20th century, fuelled by tourism and the sale of sugar to the world, had grown with vigor. Cuba ranked fifth in the hemisphere in per capita income, third in life expectancy and second in per capita ownership of automobiles and telephones. It ranked first in the number of television sets per capita in Latin America. Infant mortality was the lowest in the region and the 13th lowest in the world. Cuba's 76 percent literacy rate was the fourth highest in Latin America. It also stood 11th in the world in the number of doctors per capita and sundry private clinics and hospitals provided services for the poor. Before Castro, Cuba had 58 dailies and was eighth in the world in the number of radio stations. Its income distribution compared well with that of other Latin American societies. A flourishing middle class promised prosperity and social mobility.[1] Consequently, the obvious questions arise: Why Cuba? and Was the Revolution even necessary?

The answer to the first question is as simple as saying because Fidel Castro was Cuban, and that his enormous political, oratorical, dissemblance and leadership skills, and his all-consuming, life-long quest for power made the Revolution happen. The answer to the second question is an unequivocal no.

Fidel Castro. Who is this man who dared assume for the Cuban people that he had the right to decide most of the content and purpose of their lives? Who was he to assume that he was so Solomonic that his people would be happy to have him as their leader for the entirety of his life and to name his brother as his successor?

In some ways, his story needs no embellishment. No account of Cuba's Revolution is complete without an analysis of the man who brought off one of the most improbable feats in history: Beginning with the platoon of 12 men who survived the first attack by Batista's army near the Sierra Maestra, the mountain chain in Oriente where the rebels staked their first stand, he defeated an army thousands of times larger and better equipped, an accomplishment that can only be explained by Castro's unprecedented Machiavellian acumen and by the fact he practically wrote the book on jungle guerrilla warfare and its capacity to neutralize much larger traditional armies.

Castro is either a complex character or a simple one depending on what avenue you emphasize in the assessment. If your approach is to focus on his myriad political skills and personality traits, he is complex. But if your path is to get at his prime mover, then the man is crystal clear and simple. While he was at the University of Havana, one of his friends asked the group gathered what each wanted out of life after university. When Fidel's turn came up he said three words: "Fame and glory."[2] What was remarkable about his declaration was what he didn't say in view of his remaining biography: He didn't say "To free Cuba from the yoke of its dictators" or "To help the Cuban people gain social justice and fight for the poor." No. His was a consummate narcissistic remark. From this, you understand that the complex side of him, the one that gathered all the attributes and skills as a leader and politician, was subservient to his narcissism.

I suspect the Cuban Revolution was in the end all about him and the impetus of his life: his desire for power and glory. Standing six feet three inches, he was a big man used to looking down on others all his life. And in every way he was the classic Big Man, the tribal chief that anthropologists often refer to as the most common form of government in human prehistory. His studied posturing and histrionic, often pompous and, needless to say, long-winded oratory rounds out the profile of a soul desperate to appear to be more than what he is. Yet, for many who fell under his spell, it obviously worked. Herbert Mathews, the *New York Times* reporter who went to the Sierra Maestra to interview Fidel in February 1957, wrote: "The personality of the man is overpowering. It was easy to see his men adored him ... he was an educated, dedicated fanatic, a man of ideals, of courage, and of remarkable qualities of leadership ... one got a feeling that he is now invincible."[3] He was not the only one taken by Castro's magnetic personality, a personality that he likely nurtured throughout his life in order to dominate those around him.

His capacity for dissemblance contributed much to his success as a politician. Castro's performance for the Herbert Mathews interview was a tour de force of subterfuge. He understood what the American reporter's visit meant: Mathews would tell the American people, their government and the world if what he saw in the Sierra Maestra was a ragtag platoon of ill-equipped rebels (the truth) or the inception of a well-organized small army (the lie). The latter perception might tip the Americans into supporting him and eschewing Batista as a lost cause (and the truth be told, Batista was already an embarrassment for the U.S. who would soon cut off his supply of weapons). So, Fidel had Raúl tell Mathews he had to wait while Fidel hiked in from another (nonexistent) camp. Meanwhile Raúl marched the same 18 men, all the followers they had, in front of Mathews in different attire and formations to give the impression they were many more. Then during the interview Fidel had a sweaty and agitated messenger burst in the room bearing a message from an also make-believe "Second Column." Castro throughout the interview exaggerated the number of his supporters and created the impression his men were spirited and Batista's demoralized.[4]

The subsequent sterling report published in the *New York Times* not only made Castro an international figure, but also an almost foregone victor. Before the interview, Batista had propagated a fiction that Castro had been killed in the first skirmish, but the photograph Mathews had taken of himself and Castro belied it. Mathews' overestimate of the size of Castro's forces was all many needed to throw themselves behind the movement. Very significant was Castro's assurance to Mathews that "You can be sure that we have no animosity toward the United States and the American people ... we are fighting for a democratic Cuba and an end to the dictatorship."[5]

Much has been speculated about whether Castro was always a

"communist" and intended from the beginning to deceive the Cuban people and the world about his intentions or if he first intended being a social democrat but was forced toward communism by the way the United States reacted to the Revolution. I believe the truth was the former.

One fact is that Castro always resented U.S. influence in Cuba. In June 1958 he wrote to one of the many women in his life that "once this struggle is finished I will begin the real struggle of my life, the fight I will wage against the United States. I believe that is my true destiny."[6] Another is that in his gangster days at the University of Havana he read Marx, Engels and Lenin and that, although he always had associated himself with leftist movements, he never declared he had been a communist before he finally proclaimed to the world in December 1961 "*Soy Marxista-Leninista*." Still another was that his brother Raúl and Che Guevara were avowed communists even before they were in the Sierra Maestra and one may well speculate that they were a continuous bug in his ear on the subject—if not the other way around or a two-way street. In any event, because of the general stigma attached to communism and the anathema it meant to the Americans, Castro knew all along that he must distance himself from it for as long as possible until he consolidated absolute power over the island. Had he divulged his true intentions prematurely, Cuba's middle and higher classes and many, if not most, in the lower classes never would have supported him.

This fiction had to be upheld especially during his trip to the U.S. in April 1959, four months after Batista had fled. Castro's disdain for his hosts was evident from his attire on arrival and during his visit—army boots and olive green army fatigues, a bizarre way to dress for a visiting leader, especially during the 1950s, a time when practically everyone was in a suit. At the Council on Foreign Relations, he was grilled about reports that both his brother and Che Guevara were communists and he denied they were such.

When they met for three hours, he again denied he was a communist to Vice President Richard Nixon, who encouraged him to hold elections as soon as possible. Very telling was Castro's response: "The people don't want elections; in the past they produced bad governments."[7] In other words, he had already assumed the simple formula still in force: Fidel Castro = the Cuban people. Asked if he wanted foreign aid for Cuba, he refused it—another indication he wanted nothing from the States all along, except friendly terms until he consolidated his grip on the island. Had he accepted aid from America, he knew he would have become just another U.S. puppet dictator from Latin America, too lowly a role for the grandness of his vainglory. Instead, he chose to become the marionette of America's greatest enemy, the Soviet Union, a position that would always guarantee his place on the world stage (although he likely fancied he was not a Soviet puppet until it became all too apparent when, without consulting Castro, Nikita Khrushchev brokered a deal with Kennedy to remove the nuclear missiles from Cuba in exchange for the U.S. removing its missiles from Turkey. For many days afterward Castro was furious). When President Reagan sent the astute Vernon Walters to Havana in 1982 to evaluate Castro, Walters reported to the president: "We have nothing he wants—if we recognized him, he would be like the president of the Dominican Republic."[8]

Of course, the 1982 Cuba Vernon Walters encountered still counted on the Soviets' massive subsidies to sustain itself and the fall of the USSR was still years away. Today's Cuba is in a much more precarious position. Age and disease have turned Fidel Castro into a shadow of his former self. Raúl Castro, a far humbler man, is in power. And the Venezuela of Chávez and Maduro, whose subsidies to Cuba ebb as their debacle plays itself out, will soon implode. Indeed, things were quite different when in December 2014, President Obama reestablished diplomatic relations with Cuba.

Unlike many Cuban Americans, I was glad to hear the news. When over 50 years of embargo, 10 presidents, sundry assassination attempts on Castro, the fall of the Soviet Union and the subsequent "Special Period" of the 1990s have not done away with communism in Cuba, it might just mean the U.S. hasn't been trying the right approach. In the first place, talking is better than not talking, for the former creates the possibility of change that the latter does not. And if alienation, antagonism and ostracism haven't worked, maybe it's high time to try engagement. After all, if you're engaged in your community, you've thrown your lot in it and will tend to fall in line, for what is good for the community is good for you. This tendency is no different for countries. The U.S. should attempt to make itself indispensable to Cuba by linking their economies, a relationship wherein the U.S. has enormous advantage and leverage, for Cuba will need the U.S. far more than the converse.

The proximity of 90 miles will engender a flood of grassroots influence, largely from the U.S. to Cuba instead of the other way around since most Cubans don't have enough money to travel. Cuba and America share a long history and have a great deal more cultural similarities (Latino and Cuban-American culture, Catholicism, music, dance, baseball, boxing, the War of Independence from Spain, proximity, Hemingway, and so on) than Cuba has had with its far-flung allies. After all, Cubans and Russians were always at best an odd couple. The recognition of their affinities through mutual re-exposure will be the foundation of reciprocal acceptance and an avenue for gradual change, not only for Cubans but also for Americans. Cubans will see that contrary to what they have been told, Americans are by and large a tolerant, friendly, decent, hard-working people and Americans will surely be seduced by the grace and *simpatía* of the Cuban people. There have never been two cultures that can grow more from their rapprochement. Each has great lessons to impart to the other.

Besides, Raúl Castro, unlike his brother, has manifested economic flexibility. While paying lip service to rigid Marxist principles, a few years ago he declared that about half a million citizens would become *porsucuentistas*, or on-your-own-workers. Many of these became entrepreneurs in small businesses that have sprung up since then. He has allowed unofficial foreign travel as well as the purchase and sale of houses and cars, although it must be said that hardly anyone in Cuba has the money to take advantage of these initiatives. At any rate, Cuba seems to be already on the right track.

The U.S. should outright rescind the embargo, thereby disarming Castro morally and politically—morally because Cuba will no longer enjoy the high ground of the long-suffering David to the bully Goliath, and politically because the Castros will no longer be able to blame the embargo for what are their own economic failings. Many Cuban expatriates will say that if the embargo is removed, also removed will be the leverage to force change. But that is the problem, *forcing* things.

The hard and heavy hand only encourages entrenchment and is conducive to the political exploitation of nationalist fervor. In his decision, President Obama displayed courage and vision and I hope that Congress will follow his lead with the elimination of the embargo. The U.S. needs a measure of Zen in its international policy—it needs sometimes to "lose a battle in order to win the war."

Throughout the memoir, I use terms like mulatto or mulatta that may seem archaic or even politically incorrect to especially the American reader. The origin of this perception by the reader springs from the way views of what is "black" differed in British and Latin America. The former's approach was more separatist, absolute and unyielding. The latter's approach was more inclusive and flexible and allowed for generational social "ascent." In British America no degrees of blackness arose; one is black even if one has a mostly white phenotype. This was in line with the segregationist approach to race relations in British America. In Latin America, however, arose degrees of blackness, a mulatto being a mixed-race, light-skinned black who had more status in the traditional racist sense. This perception was in line with the strategy of *blanqueamiento*[9] or whitening that became the scheme of domination (a bit of the old "can't beat 'em, so join 'em" approach). In Cuba, a black person would attempt to marry a lighter skinned mate in order to "improve the race" and gain a higher status for the offspring. Both perceptions are racist vestiges that everyone still employs in everyday speech today and have become culturally ingrained in English and Spanish. When I was in Cuba I used the Latino one because, well, I was in Cuba and it is part of my culture.

In 2007, as the current president was being elected, I received as a gift a cool black cat I felt compelled to name Obama. Obama in most ways is as fearless as her namesake except for when it comes to thunder and lightning, in the presence of which, fearing for at least one of her nine lives, she runs headlong and cowers into the safest place my house affords: the concrete bay under the sink for the kitchen stove's gas cylinder. There's no persuading her to come out until the thunder has stopped for a good long while and then she emerges fog-like "on little cat feet and moves on in silent haunches." I wish at these times that I could explain to her about Ben Franklin and his discovery that lightning was electricity or at least that it was just Thor hammering away in Valhalla, or Zeus casting down thunderbolts from Olympus. But alas she's a cat, and she will die some sad day, like the great majority of humanity before Thor, Zeus and Franklin, afraid of thunder and lightning.

Writing this memoir turned into a kind of therapy for my spirit. Through writing it, a certain symmetry, a controlling idea regarding my life that I was unaware of before emerged. It soothed and quieted something at my core. As I pondered the reason, it finally did not surprise me, for finding an explanation, a coherence or a pattern that "illuminates the dark" is one of the most ancient of human acts and it tends to quiet our disquiet, to soothe our fears. Therefore, finding coherence in my life through the act of writing the memoir perhaps assuaged a profound anxiety I was unaware of until the final paragraph. Fear may very well be the oldest, the most basic, the founding emotion. We come into the world afraid and, if we're conscious at the time, leave it afraid. Since ancient days, we have done much to appease fear, but what most soothes, whether true or not, is what explains away things.

In a way, I wrote this for me and it made me stronger or at least it felt so because it answered so many questions about myself, but in another way I wrote it for you. I've tried in my fashion to explain much through this short work and I would be very happy if at the end of it you came away a little more confident about the world and a little less afraid.

Day One

Flying over Havana near midnight on the Fourth of July, the great city looked dim for its 500 years and 2 million people. I hadn't seen it in 50 years, since 1962, and I'd stay there for the next 10 days to secure a new birth certificate, the originals of which I had lost somewhere, sometime in my travels over the world. The trip would once and for all prove or disprove what I had known from personal experience as a boy and heard or read about my country from both sides of the great ideological canyon, The Great Divide, the island is to so many. One canyon wall reads: "A ruthless dictator took power in 1959 on the pretext of eliminating the previous ruthless dictator and creating a democracy, but instead nationalized foreign companies, abolished private property and enterprise, imprisoned or exiled the professional class and silenced all opposition, creating a totalitarian communist state." The other wall says: "A great revolutionary overthrew a corrupt dictator, rid the country of the exploitative colonialism of foreign companies and the American Mafia, established universal education and health care and created a Mecca of socioeconomic egalitarianism and human dignity." There are two sides to every story and in Havana I would see both for myself.

With symbolic perception, I packed Dostoevsky's *Notes from Underground* in my carry-on for the flight from San José, Costa Rica, and headed for the country of my birth. After all, Che Guevara thought the alienated, tortured character of this classic represented one of the ideological complaints about capitalism that he unleashed on the world: the dehumanization and estrangement inherent in the profit motive that turns people into cogs of the great money-making wheel. His is one of the central arguments that attempts to validate communism: that humanity should be guided by the motive of morality and justice toward others, indeed a beautiful concept (Christians would say, the central message of Christianity), but one that must withstand the scrutiny of reality in one of the last places that still clings to communism. I aimed to cast aside all prejudice and discover if the system worked and if it did what it purported to do.

Absolute objectivity is a pipe dream. As you will see, the thread of discourse will favor not *La Revolución*. But it is an excusable position in view of the universal recognition that the regime enforces a totalitarian state, a form of government whose egregiousness requires no objective rigor to reject it as one of the worst consequences to befall a society.

Nevertheless, I had to try against this background to remain objective, for only through this will the reader perceive the narrative as coming from an educated person instead of a semi-schooled fanatic. Compounding the problem of objectivity, memories of the four years my family lived under the regime would come to me, evoked by places and experiences in Havana—memories of how the Revolution withered and dispersed my family.

My best source of information about the state of affairs on the island would come from a group that had the least to complain about because, as I was to learn, its members were among the *nouveau riche* of Cuba. The reason I was able to gather so much from this group was that whenever I talked to one of their own, no one else was around to hear us, we were always ambulant and felt completely safe from the ears of the state. If you've not guessed it, this group was the taxi drivers. But especially helpful was a bicycle taxi (or *bicitaxi)* driver whom I hired for a few days.

An inevitable consequence of my observations of Cuba's sociopolitical situation was to contrast it to that of the United States. After all, here are two societies next to each other, yet from different ideological planets. The juxtaposition invites a fresh look at much that we take for granted in America and an honest examination of our own way of life.

I arrived at midnight along with the fifth of July. José Martí International Airport, formerly known as Rancho Boyeros International, was the undistinguished maze of steel tubes and high ceilings typical of modern airports. What set it apart was the red paint covering all the tubes, a clear message I was entering a communist country. I walked to the immigration booth where the agent inserted a visa in my passport, which she did not stamp, a favor to all Americans that visit the island. I walked to the baggage claim, waited and began to reminisce. Fifty years ago there was also no question my family was *leaving* a communist totalitarian state...

It struck me how quiet, indeed how funereal, Rancho Boyeros International Airport was that day. The quiet was broken only by loudspeaker announcements, but the rest was all whispers and shuffles. This was the only airport I would ever visit where the staff visibly hated the passengers. There was a peculiar divide between the airport's agents and its clients. Although they were from the same country, each was a stranger to the other and no one unaware of the deep structure of the moment could have guessed they were all together Cubans. The passengers, clean cut and decent, looked as if they were going to an upscale nightclub, the men in their best suit and the women in their favorite cocktail dress. My brother and I wore our navy blue First Communion suits in order to make more room in the one suitcase each was allowed to bring. I remember feeling quite the little man. Meanwhile, the staff was unkempt and informally dressed or in olive green fatigues. Many wore the ubiquitous shaggy rebel beard. But there was a difference in manner and attitude as well; the passengers, refined and reserved, the staff, coarse in gesture and expression. They didn't look at us; they glowered. Rather than speak, it seemed, they spit. It was as if, less than passengers, we were interlopers in a world we meant to exit. Everyone was on a one-way ticket and everyone knew everyone was; it was an obvious, but oddly tacit, conspiracy to leave. But because the *barbudos*, the bearded ones, held the key to the last gate, we stood the abuse with impassive dignity.

At one of the desks lined up in front of the entrance, my father presented the visas and passports. The agent looked at each passport and then deadpanned each of us, matching photo with face. He ticked his clipboard four times. Pointing with his head, he said, "Go through there to the waiting room."

"And the tickets?" father asked.

"Later," he snapped, handing back the passports, looking ahead at nothing.

The waiting room was hot and full of people sitting and fanning themselves. Men in olive green stood at the doors, Kalashnikovs pointed down. We sat down and looked around trying to figure out what next. Nobody talked. Instead, they leaned forward or whispered in the ear of someone nearby. A woman appeared out one door that led to another room and called out names of women on a clipboard. The women, some of them girls, got up and followed her into the room. As the door opened I glimpsed a screen that blocked the view inside the room. A few minutes later a man emerged from the adjacent room and called out males, who stood and followed him into that room. We were waiting to be strip-searched.

Without turning his head, the dapper man next to father whispered from behind his newspaper, "You didn't bring the title to any properties, I hope."

Father started to turn his head towards him before catching himself and said in a ventriloquist's whisper, "Yes. Why?"

"Because they'll cancel your ticket to make sure they've confiscated it and to tidy their books, which are a disaster. You'd better get rid of it before they search you."

"*Mil gracias, amigo.*"

Facundo turned to Consuelo and whispered in her ear. Her eyes widened for an instant and she blushed. Then she nonchalantly covered her purse with her jacket. After a minute, the jacket began to move up and down slightly. Then she looked to the right and moved the jacket to her left side. The purse was now exposed, but the jacket was minutely moving up and down again on her left, while she kept looking right. The movement under the jacket stopped, and then she replaced the garment on the purse while her eyes swept the room back to the left. Maybe it was just my mother; maybe it's that women have a knack for the spy game, but the fact is that Consuelo had successfully stuffed under the seat cushion the title, which had been brought along in the vague hope that the farm could be some day reclaimed.

About an hour later they called our names. Consuelo was ushered into the women's room while we were strip-searched in the men's. They found nothing on the list of things that would compel them to cancel our tickets. Searching through our luggage, they found nothing that interested them, but I saw how they took things of value from the suitcases of the other men who had come before us. On a table in the middle of the room there were flat boxes full of valuables that they had confiscated: rings, watches, cameras, chains, bracelets, binoculars, cufflinks, tiepins, money. Then they took our suitcases and put them on a wheeled rack. While my father was still putting his pants back on, the man who'd searched him said, "By the way, you have to hand over the money in your wallet." Pops knew better than to argue, so he removed the bills and handed them over. "You have any more money?" he demanded.

"Just the change in my coin purse," said Facundo.

"Hand it over." Those coins were the last things they took from us. Years later at university in America, I would read about the Jews and their plight with the Nazis and would feel a kinship with them that was profound and disturbing.

The waiting room led to another large chamber with floor to ceiling windows beyond which we could see the Constellation, a four-engine airliner with the sky blue initials KLM on the side. There was a counter on the left under a sign that said TICKETS. Father went up to it and handed the annoyed agent our passports. The man stamped them and gave him the four boarding passes that were the currency of our freedom. There was a line already forming in front of the door that led to the tarmac where the big plane sat. We went up to the tail of the line and shuffled our way to the last agent, whose job it was to check the passports and the tickets. Then suddenly we were in the blazing sun of Havana on our way to the stairs that went up to the plane. As we climbed in silence, I heard a woman murmur, "*Casi.*" "Almost."

It was not until we were over water that the 70 or so passengers relaxed enough to converse. It started when one gentleman nearby said aloud to his wife, "Honey, I think we can talk now." Many laughed at this and then they all got going. I heard the man in front say to his wife, "Never in my life did I imagine one day I'd have to keep my mouth shut to survive." There was talk of the relief of speaking freely, some of the loss of everything and some about hopes and dreams in America. Almost as soon as we reached 18,000 feet we started descending, a mere 15 minutes into the flight. When the wheels touched down the passengers could no longer contain their emotion. "Freedom!" "Free at last!" they shouted standing up and hugging in tears. Gathering us about his arms, father said, "*Consuelo, muchachos, ¡esto es la libertad!*"

15

"This is freedom!" Outside some fell to their knees and kissed the ground. Upon landing, we tried to find the dapper man who had warned us about the title, but for one reason or another we never found him. I remember asking my father, "*Papi, qué le pasó a la nieve?*" "What happened to the snow?" For some reason known only to poets and the young, I had gotten the impression that all of America was a land of snow. My father laughed aloud and said, "My son we've only traveled 90 miles to the north!"

I got my luggage and looked for an exchange booth. I had brought euros with me knowing that dollars are exchanged with a 10 percent charge. At the teller, I counted out 100 euros for which I received 121 Cuban convertible units or CUC (pronounced something like "cook" in the Spanish acronym), the same as the euro-dollar exchange. The teller chuckled when I asked her, "What are these the famous Cuban cooks (*cocineros cubanos*)?"

Cuba has two national currencies, the CUC and the peso. Neither currency functions outside the island. A few years ago the government withdrew the dollar from circulation. The CUC, used for tourism and for luxury items, is worth 24 pesos, which are doled out to Cubans for their labor. Both currencies are interchangeable on the island. In other words, you can pay in CUC and get pesos in change and vice versa. The regime introduced the CUC in 2004 when the dollar was declared money non grata and a 10 percent charge was imposed on its exchange.

Outside, cabbies waited to take passengers to Havana. A tall black man stepped up and said, "Havana. Thirty minutes. 20 CUC" (only he pronounced it "sirty"). I knew that it was a good price, so I said, "*Vámonos.*" On the way, I told the driver about my mission to get a birth certificate. He was very helpful, in an impassive, almost resigned tone, telling me what civil registry I had to go to the next day and what to do if they told me it would take more time than I had.

"Just slip the agent a little tip for speeding it up. It never fails and nobody takes it personally. They need the money."

"How much is a decent tip?"

"I'd say about five CUC should be enough."

Thinking about what it would take to bribe an official in Costa Rica I said, "I imagined it would be more. Maybe thirty."

"A typical salary here is a measly 15, 20 CUC's. Thirty is twice a month's salary for them. Way too much. Things have changed since the last time you were here."

At the Casa Nilma in Old Havana they were waiting for my arrival. Nilma, the middle-aged woman who was the owner, welcomed me and in an old rickety elevator led me up to the top floor. On the way she explained that we had to be quiet lest we wake up the three Colombians staying in one of the rooms of the "suite." The eighth-floor suite was airy and spacious. Crossing the big living/dining room, she ushered me to my room on the far right corner of the suite. It was ample and had a balcony. Handing me the keys, she whispered, "Ana, my maid will come tomorrow and make you breakfast. What time is convenient?" I said that seven would be good and we bid goodnight.

Alone, I went to a balcony on the suite's other corner. One side faced the street, the other, Havana Bay and the Malecón. I could see that Casa Nilma sat atop one of the tallest buildings in the area. Below, along the narrow dim street, I made out the provocative figures of young women, at this hour still plying their ancient trade. I looked at the building across and realized that the floor of the top floor had become the present roof. Beyond the tangle of rooftops flowed the channel leading to Havana Harbor on the right. I looked left and, just like 50 years before, Morro Castle guarded the entrance to the harbor. Its great lighthouse, rising above the ramparts on the point, winked at me in welcome.

I couldn't sleep well that night, thoughts spinning through my mind without letup. Would they still have my birth certificate after nearly 60 years? Why should they care about an exile who left as a boy? After all, I was an enemy of the State by association with my parents and family. Would I run into trouble with the State? Would they mire me in red tape? Would they be willing and helpful? Or would they be resentful of me and all I represented to them? They call us *gusanos*, worms, those who left and still leave for America and freedom. Such is the extent of their scorn.

It takes courage to leave behind all you ever had, all the people you have ever known and a culture that's part of your being to go with nothing left to you in the world to a strange land and an unknown life. And if you do it by crossing one of the most shark infested straits in the world in a leaky boat, it takes great inner strength and pluck, but if you don't have these in you, you need something that will compensate for their lack: despair. *Gusanos*? We who made it know better. We know what it is to become an American, to arrive young or old in a new land, to change with it or fail, to learn English, to play it their way until you triumph in their way of triumph: to stand alone and brash before the world and say "Here I am, folks! This is what I have to offer. Take it or leave it!"

How well we mastered the lessons of America, my brother and I. We took the learned road to come up from that day when we arrived with our First Communion suit on and a suitcase. He became a physician and I, a teacher. We became boys of summer, of American football in the fall, of hockey and of basketball in winter. Almost forgetting Spanish, we learned English better than our American friends. We fell in love with American girls and danced to the rhythms of American music. We tempered our wishes with the yield of our work. By a mix of the years and all the acts that fill them with life in America, we became Americans. My mind wandered back, following these thoughts, to slipstream behind them into sleep, back to when America to us was just, just a womb…

The first few weeks, we stayed with Aunt Beatriz, Consuelo's youngest sister, and her family, who for some years had already been living in Miami. Initially, the U.S. government helped with $100 a month and food rations like flour, butter, grease, powdered milk, rice, beans, eggs, and a curious canned meat called Spam. The aid lasted while the head of the family remained unemployed. My father, however, had something to offer his hosts. Because on arrival in Miami he was already practically bilingual, in no time he landed a job as desk clerk of the Carlisle Hotel in Miami Beach. The Carlisle management gave us a cut rate to stay in one of their rooms and we moved into a spacious hotel room with a view of the Atlantic.

But at that time South Beach was no country for young men. What was most striking about Miami Beach was the age of the inhabitants, who tended to walk slowly or with the help of a cane. Of course, the

South Beach of the early sixties was a far cry from the glitz and glamor of its later renaissance. The Art Deco hotels that lined the Ocean Front had been constructed in the twenties and thirties and now they were as much in decadence as the people that inhabited them. Most were retired Jews from New York and the north, but many had found retirement in South Beach a pleasant alternative to a Europe still in reconstruction or an insecure Israel. The accommodations were cheap, the view, elegant, and the weather was nothing air conditioning couldn't fix. There was a certain irony in that South Beach was one way or another being populated by exiles. With its perfect beach and groomed lawns along the palm-tree lined Ocean Drive contrasting with the colorful streamlined, exotic paint-chipped hotels, South Beach was a sort of decaying Cockaigne for the dispossessed. The old Jews, deprived by history and of their youth, and the younger Cubans, deprived of country and possessions, had found a common ground.

On our part, Facundito and I could not be happier living in front of the ocean. We'd go to the beach every day and swim and play in the sand. Facundito discovered that they would give you two pennies for every empty glass bottle you brought to a store, so our first job in America was collecting soda bottles on the beach. Two dozen bottles and the enterprising new Americans had enough to go to the matinee on Collins Avenue. We went to the beach so much the sun turned us blond and black. Like all kids, we found a way to make friends, mostly Cuban children of exiles like us. Those days were a blur of fun: the jumps off the pier, the sand ball fights, the snorkeling, the sand castles, the sand burials, the water fights, the dives off the shoulders and the beach trench warfare. Then there were games with no names like the hold-your–breath-underwater-the-longest game and the pull-down-someone's-pants-underwater game and there were the water jousts where I was always battling from my brother's shoulders. Of course, all this was before we discovered beach balls. These days of entropy were some of my happiest in America.

In the meantime, father was applying to universities throughout the United States. After many attempts, the following year he secured a position as Spanish and political science professor at a branch of the University of Loyola in Chicago. The university paid for our trip and we moved north.

Ten years later we still lived in the Chicago area in the summer of 1972. Playing itself out for us was the American Dream and all its symbols: the house in the suburbs, the two cars, the televisions, the phones, the washer and dryer, the stereo, the microwave, the lawn and the mower—today all of it the flotsam and jetsam of our days gone by. The Vietnam and Cold Wars raged on TV among images of hippies, protests, ICBM's, marijuana and rock 'n' roll. An odd "revolution," or so they called it, was brewing in America. The media often gave it other names: the youth movement, the civil rights movement, the feminist movement, even the sexual revolution. In reality, what was happening was no revolution at all, just a reaffirmation of the world's longest existing revolution, the American Revolution, founded on the principles of the primacy of the individual and the mistrust of government. "Americans had lost touch with themselves; they're just getting a second skin," said father one day.

By 1972 Facundito, or his adopted Americanized name, Frank, and I had molted into Americans who spoke English to each other and Spanish to the old folks. We played American football in winter, baseball in summer and flirted it seemed only with blondes we fondled in a Plymouth we shared every other Saturday. During the summer breaks, we worked at Inland Steel, a major steel making company in northwest Indiana. These jobs would help pay for our univer-

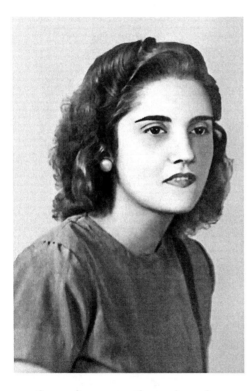

Consuelo, my mother, when she was young, circa 1935, still unaware of the maelstrom that was to come. She never had to cook or clean or labor in her life, until after the Revolution. She arrived in Miami at 47 and never missed a beat.

sity careers. My brother, a freshman at university, wanted to be a doctor and was a serious, "straight A" student, while I wanted to travel the world, but had a vague notion of how to do it. I was also vague about my studies. Unlike Frank, I excelled only at what interested me and was nonchalant about whatever did not. The age-old disease, youth's ancient feeling of immortality, had a hold on me. And of course, I had discovered a distracting, undue universe in a woman's mere angle, curve, or line in place.

Consuelo was the incurable Cuban housewife, with her Creole cooking, her incessant cleaning frenzies, and her arms akimbo at the slightest male mischief. Her life in America took place mostly at home. She oil painted in her spare time, creating impressionistic works, whose style we kidded her was due to her poor eyesight. Hers were the thousand heroic little daily tasks that comprise the pillar that is a good wife to a husband and a mother to two sons. But she paid a price for the insularity of the home: she never quite learned English past the intermediate level and she was the least Americanized of the family. Father, who I now called Pops, would from time to time declare a new law of the house, "Heretofore, Spanish shall not be spoken at home in order to improve the English of your mother!" This law and its many forms would work for about a day, after which convenience tacitly made it disappear. But Consuelo never did stop trying to learn her English and she finally learned it well enough to read the newspaper and function with it outside the home. Yes, she was a heroine, an everyday heroine, who gave her life for us, just as surely as a Marine diving on a grenade to save his buddies, but she dove on that grenade every day of her life for us...

DAY TWO

I rose with the sun along with the three Colombians who were headed to Varadero. They were young and excited at the prospect of the famous beach. As arranged, Ana showed up at seven. She was a kind middle-aged woman whose dominant expression was a strained smile that hid some internal pain. She came to fix me breakfast the next few days and I would come to know Ana, her hidden political orientation and the origin of her pain as each day she made me breakfast and shared the table with me. The Colombians were in too much of a hurry so they skipped breakfast and went out the door promising to return in five days. Left alone with Ana, she served me a breakfast of eggs and fruit and *galletas*, Cuban crackers.

"I understand you're Cuban but that you left a long time ago."

"Yes, 50 years ago my family went to the United States. I'm back to get my birth certificate." I noticed she was looking at the Nikon camera I had set on the table.

"Do you like photography?" I asked. "Not so much, but my son does, he's studying to be an architect. He's really very talented, but he needs a good camera for his studies. I'm trying to get him a decent one before he goes to Spain to study. May I ask how much that one cost?"

"It was a little expensive, about a thousand dollars." Her face sank above the smile that remained only in her mouth.

"A thousand dollars! We're not so lucky here in Cuba; almost no one can afford so much, especially for a camera. You must have a good job to afford such a camera."

"The best job in the world; I'm a teacher."

"Really? I'm a teacher too! Well ... at least I was."

"Why did you give up teaching?"

"Because I couldn't make enough to live ... comfortably and also to help my son."

From this and other exchanges I understood the source of her pain: her son and her struggle to allow him to study in Europe (Spain, in an effort to boost the population had welcomed for citizenship the children and grandchildren of Spanish Creoles), where he would get a good wage for the considerable talents she was convinced were his. A few days later, having lost all hope of buying a professional camera for her son, she would ask me how much a camera "not so good as yours, but still good" would cost. When I told her, it didn't remedy the mask she had selected before the world.

Ana called Ramón, the Casa Nilma's taxi driver, to take me to the Miramar Civil Registry, where I guessed my birth certificate would be since I was born in a clinic of that Havana district. Ramón, a tall thin mulatto waited leaning on the hood of a Lada, a Russian-made compact car common in Cuba along with the East German Trabant. This was my introduction to the world of the Cuban car, by far the most important, if not, sometimes the most comical, mechanical object on the island. The car was a lumpy shadow of its former austere glory. It had been brush-painted a color that I'm still not sure participated in the spectrum, for light did not readily escape its surface. Ramón had to get in first to open the passenger door. A cloth covered what felt like bare springs under me and during the rest of the ride I had to grab the roof so as not to list toward Ramón. The interior door paneling had been removed and I finally learned about the simple levers that open a car door. When Ramón turned the ignition, it seemed a locomotive roared to life. The rest of the trip, with fumes seeping into the cab, I'd now and then stick my face out the window like a large dog. "*Este carro es muy simpático*," I said. Ramón laughed and thanked me.

"*Gracias*. I guess to you it's charming, but here this is normal."

"How old is it?"

"It's a '73, so you can imagine. I inherited it from my father, but it's not really mine. Not yet anyway."

"How can it not be yours if you inherited it?"

"It's technically the government's and it technically didn't even belong to my father. He got it from a Russian who brought it over in the old days and it's still in the Russian's name."

"How did he get it from the Russian? He buy it?"

"Are you kidding? Even if the state allowed it, nobody in Cuba has

23

money to buy a car. No, the Russian left it to him when he went back to Russia. He was some big shot; my father was his driver."

"But why is it still in the Russian's name?"

"I guess it's just easier for the state to keep track of their cars. So look, all cars, except the pre-'59 Americans, are in the name of the last owner right after the '59 Revolution or the last Russian or the last Czechoslovakian, Romanian, East German who brought one. You see all those American cars?" I looked at the steady stream of 50's Chevrolets, Oldsmobiles, Fords, Buicks and Chryslers—all in varying states of maintenance, from beautifully restored to junk yard state. "Those are the only ones that can be bought and sold with titles, but then the only ones who can buy them are taxi drivers. But guess what, they recently announced that soon post–'59 cars will have their titles transferred to their current caretaker and that we'll no longer need the special permit from the government to buy any car. It's one of Raúl's changes. So this car will finally be mine."

"But Ramón, this car is on its last legs; it had better be pretty soon."

"No way! This car's an oak! Well ... the mechanical part that is. That I take good care of, otherwise I can't work, but I'll be damned if I'll pour money into the body before I know it's in my name!"

I had to laugh, then asked, "Why are taxi drivers the only ones that can buy cars?"

"Oh, I guess I didn't explain it well.... Here the taxi drivers are the rich."

Later, I reflected on the implications of this conversation. One was Ramón's words, "...but I'll be damned if I'll pour money into the body before I know it's in my name!" an inadvertent admission of humanity's self-interested core, at odds with communism's founding principle. Here was a man born and raised into a system that from the very beginning taught him to resign his selfhood for society's sake. Yet he blurted out something that negated all that indoctrination. "Here the taxi drivers are the rich" implied the creation of a topsy-turvy society, engendered by more than 50 years of a command economy.

The great majority of the 300,000 vehicles on the island, most of them in Havana, are taxis and, once you understand the reason, you realize that it could not be any other way. The average Cuban's salary is around $15 to $20 a month; $25 to $35 is the highest bracket, com-

A restored 1956 Chevrolet Bel Air. "Here the taxi drivers are the rich."

posed of professionals. Not only is buying a car way out of reach of such salaries, the price of gas at a state gas station is $1.20 per liter. To fill the tank, a doctor would have to invest almost her entire salary. Needless to say, almost no one uses the official gas stations and instead buys cheap gas stolen from the government. Running up and down one of the main boulevards all day and night collecting ride-sharing passengers each way, a taxi *colectivo* charging about 40 Cuban cents per passenger can earn $5 on a good day. Chauffeurs can also hire out the taxi exclusively, for which they can charge the same as in many countries. A chauffeur who applies himself can earn a few hundred dollars a month, a king's ransom in Cuba. This is the reason we see the grand American cars of the 40's and 50's still on the road. No matter what the cost, it's worth the effort and expense to maintain them.

Havana's scenery streamed by. The city today is light in traffic for its wide avenues and boulevards. Not once did I see a traffic jam and rush hours don't exist. Havana was built for a more prosperous, busier and more bustling society whose stately bones and arteries endure. As

I looked at the listless pedestrians it was hard to imagine they could have constructed such a monument. But even with few cars on the roads, after about a week in Havana I developed a hacking dry cough from the diesel and black market semi-refined gasoline that they burn.

Ramón dropped me off at the Miramar Civil Registry. As it turned out, the annoyed civil servants there didn't find my certificate and suggested I go to the one in Vedado, the sprawling old upper-middle-class district west of Old Havana. I walked to Calle Linea, one of the main four-lane east-west boulevards and hailed a *colectivo* that let me off near the Vedado registry. Here, some charming and attentive ladies dropped everything to help me, first by checking their own archives and then, as my heart was sinking, by making phone calls to other registries. The first call resulted in another failure. The lady looked at my expression and said, "*Tranquilo, no te preocupes*" ("Relax, don't worry,"). Phoning another registry, she repeated my name then my parents' and grandparents' and waited. A few minutes passed while she drummed her fingers on the desk. Then she took down some numbers and hung up. Looking up at me she said, "Bingo. It's your lucky day. Your certificate is at the Havana Central Registry!" I sighed in relief and thanked them. They told me the certificate would be here after lunch and that I should buy a certification stamp at the local post office and bring it back.

After getting the stamp, I went to have lunch at La Maison Française, a once elegant, now paint-chipped restaurant with a veranda facing Calle Linea. My mind was made up about what I was going to eat: the world-famous Cuban Sandwich, a delicacy I hadn't tasted for 50 years. A Cuban Sandwich is composed of three slices of ham, three slices roast pork, three slices of Swiss cheese, three or four slices of pickles and a generous cut of Cuban bread (or French bread), butter spread on one slice, mustard on the other. It's pressed with a hinged double hot plate until the cheese melts and it's toasty on the outsides. I told the young waiter about my minor dream and he assured me they'd do their best to make me a good one. It took 45 minutes. The bread was old, hard and crumbly; the cheese was some soggy tasteless mass that had been interrupted on the way to becoming cheese, the ham made Spam taste like pork tenderloin, there was no pork or pickle, and an oily mayonnaise slurped off the sides. I took one bite and had to put it down. In fact, I covered it with a napkin so that it would do me no further damage. The waiter returned to take the plate away. He asked how I liked it.

"Do you want the truth or would you like me to pretend?"

"Please tell the truth."

"That was the worst sandwich I ever had." He looked hurt and said he was sorry I didn't like it. "It's not your fault." I paid and left to get my certificate, wondering on the way if what I had been told about the quality of today's Cuban food was true.

In the following days, I discovered that it was. That same day, ravenous after my one bite of the sandwich, I decided to have lunch at a charming old corner restaurant near my guesthouse in Old Havana. La Republica, with its mahogany woodwork, checkered tablecloths, and bow-tied waiters in vests, was what Hemingway would have called a clean well-lighted place. I drank down the worst Cuba Libre I ever tasted (because of the cola in it) while I waited for the "pulled pork" plate recommended by the waiter. When it came it looked good. The boiled potatoes and veggies were aesthetically set and the pork seemed what you'd expect—until I started to sift through it and found bone fragments, and strings of nerves, veins and ligaments mixed in it. I managed the nausea and enjoyed what I could of the meal. I started to suspect that many Cubans have little idea of what good food is.

The Cubans I encountered in Havana were rarely overweight and at first sight appeared healthy. But when I looked at the eyes of many of the middle aged, I often saw the muddy white of the eyes that betrayed the poor diet they've endured. One of the staples of Cuban life is *"la libreta,"* the little notebook on which Cubans keep track of their monthly subsidized food rations consisting of rice, beans, cooking oil, sugar, coffee, ten eggs, and a quarter chicken per person. For most this is enough for seven to ten days. The rest of the month Cubans barter for food, eat lunch at workplace subsidized cafeterias, grow their own or buy it on the black market. While no one starves, Cubans subsist on a monotonous diet, largely lacking meat and fresh vegetables.

After lunch and a siesta, I rose to find Nilma and her son Juanito in the living room. They greeted me warmly and Nilma invited me to a dinner at the apartment the next day, an invitation I accepted as it meant I would not have to chance another meal at a restaurant. The occasion was to welcome back Nilma's childhood friend, who had married a Lebanese and moved to Beirut. Then Juanito asked if there was anything I'd like to know or places I wanted to visit. I told him how much I liked Cuban jazz. He told me of three clubs of which the nearest was El Jazz Café, so I made up my mind to go there that night. I asked Juanito how to get to the Capitol and the twenty-something drew a map directing me to El Parque Central, which straddles the famous building. Part of the directions included the square where the yacht *Granma* is sepulchered. This was the rickety vessel that Castro and his 80 followers had crashed on the rocks off Oriente province on their way to starting the Revolution some 58 years ago. Jorgito, drawing the map on a napkin, curiously said, "And here is the park where the *Granma* is exhibited; you know, the yacht that brought Fidel and his little friends to Cuba from Mexico." His mother was within earshot of the innuendo and I knew that he had said this in her defiance or with her complicity. Either way, I didn't care to press on about it, for I knew from personal experience even as a child that in Cuba, unless you're sure about who is listening, you don't really know where your mouth will land you.

After they'd left, I remained in the balcony. I looked down at the roof across the street. All the way up and down the block the roofs had disappeared long ago and the new roofs were the former top floors.

From this view, the whole area almost had the appearance

A very typical bird's-eye view in Old Havana. The former top floor is the new roof.

of German cities after World War II. The walls that used to support the roofs still stood eroding in the rain and sun. A big puddle lay in what before was someone's living room. Around the puddle drank a brood of chicks like a necklace of fuzzy pearls. The mother hen was the pendant. "So this is how they survive," I said aloud. I looked to the left toward the bay and sat down on the little sofa and saw the sun starting to sink into the Caribbean. I took shots of Morro Castle in the amber light then sat down to reflect on a man who long ago took over that bastion for his dark designs.

More than fifty years ago, Ernesto "Che" Guevara (Che was the nickname the Cuban comrades in arms had given him. Che in Argentinian Spanish means "chico" in Cuban Spanish or "buddy," "pal" or "dude" in English) had turned Morro Castle into an execution dungeon for those accused of ties to the Batista regime. I thought about how there were some admirable qualities in Guevara, his valor, leadership and heartfelt desire to stand up for the disadvantaged. But I also recognized that his intolerance for any but his own opinions and ideals, a fanaticism that led him to advocate even global thermonuclear warfare to achieve those ideals and his callous ruthlessness against those who opposed him made him a specious hero, if not a flawed and dangerous character.

In the Sierra Maestra, the mountain chain in the east where the rebels staked their first stand, he acted as the self-appointed henchman, administering death without rancor or pity to anyone even suspected of being a traitor. A pistol shot to the head; problem solved. The first time he played the role, the execution of Eutimio Guerra, he'd write in his diary that he felt fine afterward, at total peace with his conscience. He added the following excerpt from his diary (found in Jon Lee Anderson's otherwise flattering biography, *Che Guevara: A Revolutionary Life*), an excerpt so bizarre, chilling and unbecoming that it was a guarded state secret for 40 years after Guevara's death. Che wrote:

> The situation was uncomfortable for the people and so I ended the problem giving him a shot with a .32 pistol in the right side of the brain, with exit orifice in the right temporal lobe. He gasped a little while and was dead. Upon proceeding to remove his belongings I couldn't get off the watch tied by a chain to his belt, and then he [Eutimio] told me in a steady voice farther away than fear: "Yank it off, boy, what does it matter...." I did so and his possessions were now mine. We slept badly, wet and with something of asthma.

Even Jon Lee Anderson found it difficult to reconcile his generally favorable portrayal of Che with the excerpt; he wrote: "Che's narrative is as chilling as it is revealing about his personality. His matter of fact-ness in describing the execution, his scientific notation on his bullet's entry and exit wounds, suggest a remarkable detachment from violence. To Che, the decision to execute Eutimio himself was, in his own words, a way to 'end an uncomfortable situation.' As for his recollection of Eutimio's posthumous 'last words,' it is simply inexplicable and lends a surreal dimension to the grim scene."[1]

In the Sierra Maestra, several dozen men saw the lightning off his pistol muzzle but never heard its thunder. And in La Cabaña (The Hut, the castle dungeon's euphemism), hundreds met a similar fate, many, summary executions before the firing squads under his command. As Hugh Thomas wrote in his objective history of Cuba: "He was not a merciful spirit. A Cuban lawyer defending a woman accused of having

Morro Castle with its lighthouse. The cargo ship, Berulan, is entering Havana Harbor through the narrow strait between the Malecón and the cas-tle's ramparts. Che Guevara turned the fortress into an execution chamber, where hundreds faced the firing squads without due process.

had relations with the previous government recalled that Guevara in 1959 said: 'I don't know how you dare take an interest in this person.... I will have her shot... If any person has a good word for the previous government that is enough for me to have him shot.'"[2]

His was a black and white world; black was reality and white, his ideals. For this charismatic man, the first and last time that the real and ideal were one was the triumph of the Revolution. Thereafter, reality never measured up. His stubborn denial of the way of the world led him to fail at everything he attempted after the Revolution. As treasury minister (in an act illustrative of his disdain for money and, by extension, the conventions of humanity, his signature on every Cuban peso was his nickname: *Che*) then as minister of industry, as a guerrilla leader in Africa then in Bolivia—in effect, in every endeavor without Fidel Castro's vaulting talent for politics and dissemblance, he took turns in failure.[3] The Bolivian adventure may have been atonement to Fidel for Che's chastising the Soviets for abandoning Marxist principles during his visit to the Soviet Union. Almost as if assuming the role of sacrificial lamb, he proposed the Bolivian escapade to Fidel, who curiously accepted the mission from his 39-year-old asthmatic, second-in-command. Just as he had done to so many, Che ended up abandoned without trial or jury, waiting for the business end of a gun to bloom.

Yet maybe it's because he was handsome and with his long hair and beard predated the youth movement and was therefore adopted by it; maybe it was the lure of the iconic photo by Alberto Korda, The Heroic Guerrilla; or it was the romance of the victory of the underdog against all odds that was the Revolution, or the gullibility of what Lenin called "our useful idiots in the West," or simple old anti–Americanism; or maybe it was all the above, but the ironic truth is that the Argentine whose image appears worldwide on T-shirts, tattoos, coffee mugs, murals and paintings as an icon of freedom and a protector of the oppressed was a totalitarian who believed in the persuasion of violence and death to attain his absurd yet seductive ideals. These inveighed against the profit motive and the universal self-interest at the core of human behavior. Instead, he believed in developing a collective attitude to production and the concept of work as a social duty, in other words, a group-oriented moral motive for making a living. Of course, it is a nice but naïve ideology that contradicts 200,000 years of human natural selection. In every instance of its enforcement, the only way to maintain it has been through total control of education and information, turning much of the population into spies, and repressing opposing views through the threat of death or imprisonment. In order to realize the ideology, however, he believed mostly in violence. Che once wrote in his diary: "Hatred is an element of struggle; unbending hatred for the enemy, which pushes a human being beyond his natural limitations, making him into an effective, violent, selective, and cold-blooded killing machine."[4] No doubt he saw himself as that machine. In a posthumously published article written during the Cuban Missile Crisis, Guevara divulged the delusional extent of his fanaticism. He wrote: "...we must proceed along the path of liberation, even at the cost of millions of atomic victims."[5]

The young Guevara in Argentina already manifested some of the tendencies that helped shape his ultimate persona. He enjoyed shocking people and was nicknamed El Chancho, The Pig, for his penchant for rarely bathing and for wearing the same clothes for many days. His father, Ernesto Guevara Lynch, of Irish and Basque descent, referring to the young man's restlessness, once declared, "the first thing to note is that in my son's veins flowed the blood of the Irish rebels."[6] Born to a leftist, intellectual and politically active family, he had access to a broad spectrum of political and philosophical literature and early on developed "an affinity for the poor." He read eclectically and voluminously a spectrum of authors: Marx, Lenin, Faulkner, Freud, Sartre, Frost, Camus, Engels, Kafka, Darío, London, Nietzsche, Verne and Wells.[7] A life-long diarist, he maintained records of his experiences and observations until his death in the mountains of Bolivia.

In Che's *Motorcycle Diaries*, his romanticized treks through Latin America in the 1950's, he documented how his experiences shaped his ideology. In a letter to his Aunt Beatriz posted from San José, Costa Rica, Guevara spoke of traversing through the "dominions" of the United Fruit Company, which convinced him of the horror of the "capitalist octopuses." This indignation began the head-hunting tone that he adopted and was consecrated when Guevara swore on an image of the then recently deceased Joseph Stalin, "not to rest until these octopuses have been vanquished."[8] That he swore his incantation over the altar of the second greatest butcher in history (the first not being Adolf

The Heroic Guerrilla, March 5, 1960. Alberto Korda's iconic photo of Che Guevara, who was 31 at the time, was taken while Fidel gave a speech at the memorial service for the victims of the explosion of the French freighter *La Coubre* in Havana Harbor. The photo, which ironically turned into a moneymaking engine for capitalist entrepreneurs, was part of the creation of the ill-founded Guevara mystique.

Hitler, but Mao Zedong) apparently did not faze him: The young Argentine had found his ideology and it was communism. Throughout the two motorcycle trips and the one he later took ending in Mexico where he met Fidel Castro, he came to the simplistic conclusion (a very surprising one for such a well-read young man) that capitalism was evil and that Latin America was poor because North America and Western Europe were rich.[9]

That simplicity struck a chord across Latin America. The reason for the region's poverty and socio-political dysfunction now had a scapegoat on whose coattails ride the leftist semi-totalitarian movements brewing today in Bolivia, Nicaragua, Ecuador, Argentina and, of course, Venezuela. It is as if much of the region wallowed in the role of the victim. In many political discussions one hears in Costa Rica no one ever mentions us, but them, more specifically the Gringos, at the heart of their problems. Of course, this in no way helps to remedy what is at the core of the predicaments the region has faced in its past and present. As we witness the present government of Venezuela lash out at the United States' "imperialism" as the source of all the problems it has itself caused in that once self-sufficient nation, we could not have a better example of Latin America's penchant for refusing to accept blame for its dysfunction.

Never mind that the people that colonized British America went there to evade religious and political exploitation and persecution and that what characterized the colonization of Latin America was the opposite: the Spanish and Portuguese went to exploit, repress and subdue the region for its wealth. British America was colonized mainly by civilians; Latin America, by soldiers. Those that became "North Americans" wanted to build a home; those that became Latin Americans, a vast gold and silver mine. This meant that building a decent society took a back seat to creating a society of subjugation and developing healthy diversified economies took second place to mining for precious metals. When agriculture was finally addressed as an economic alternative, many colonies like Cuba were practically turned into huge farms for commodities that didn't feed the people (sugar, tobacco, rubber, and coffee) and caused them to feast or famine depending on the commodity's world price. A feudal system wherein a *hacendado* owned an enormous tract of land tilled by illiterate peasants became the economic model. The Bourbon Reforms' insistence on Iberian, rather than Creole, bureaucrats[10] to administrate the colonies helped along an already established caste system of white supremacist oligarchies at the top, followed by the mestizos, then the indigenous population and blacks. The plan of many early arrivals to Spanish America was to prove one's mettle as a soldier or bureaucrat in the eyes of the Crown, accumulate some ill-gotten wealth and retire to the peninsula with perhaps a higher position or even a title of nobility.

The aftereffects of the militaristic and exploitative approach to colonization prevailed. Instead of the meritocracy of the United States, the establishment of white oligarchies led to widespread nepotism, stifling inventiveness, development and enterprise. A general ambiance endured of abandon and carelessness, a lack of attention to detail and seriousness in the emerging, uprooted, makeshift cultures. It was almost as if the Iberian monarchies had set up the entire continent to be treated and to treat itself like a rental.

The region failed to develop unassailable and lasting institutions. The army became not one institution among many, but The Institution. Whoever controlled the army assumed power, hence, the innumerable coups that have plagued the region. Just in the 20th century there were over 300 coups d'état in Latin America.[11] The Crown sent to its colonies low-level bureaucrats, paid them a poor wage, yet expected incommensurate results along with banquets, parades and tours for visiting dignitaries. Sometimes the bureaucrats paid themselves too high a salary. Both tendencies led to the only way out for the bureaucrats: graft.[12] In Latin America, graft became a tacit cultural trait at every level of society. There is even a proverb dedicated to this penchant: *La ley se cumple, pero no se obedece.* You abide by the law, but you don't obey it. When graft becomes cultural and the law turns into something to be winked at, when it is not what you know, but who you know, apathy and hopelessness tends to dwell in the minds of those that want to do well for themselves and society. Guevara never considered this background in his assessment of Latin America's dysfunction and chose to target the Americans and Europeans as the sole cause—hardly the mental workings of the man referred to by Jean Paul Sartre as "the most complete human being of our time."

At about 9 o'clock in front of the Malecón, I suddenly turned around because of a whistle. The man who'd whistled had done so to get the attention of someone across the street, but the first person I saw upon turning around was a well-dressed man with a clipped mustache who looked away from me when I turned around. I stuck my hand out to hail a taxi to take me to the Jazz Café. A pod-like, two seat taxi pulled over and I got in. The driver, a corpulent white man who seemed to fill more than half the car's interior, exchanged pleasantries with me before I asked him point blank, "What do you think of the Revolution?"

"The Revolution? A bunch of crap. And I'm one of the lucky ones. Compared to the rest, my main complaint is that I don't have a bigger car. But I tell you looking back my biggest mistake was not defecting while I was conscripted at 18 to fight in Africa. I might have done something with my life instead of driving around like a madman all day to make a living."

"What do the unlucky ones complain about?"

"Ridiculous salaries, what to eat, spending your life pretending, and generally having to lick the ass of the regime for every advantage in life. The real economy here is unofficial. You wouldn't believe how much stealing from the government goes on, corruption. It's all crap! Here's the Jazz Café."

The building's curved façade faced El Malecón, the miles-long half-moon seawall before Havana Bay, its great promenade now crowded with young people partying. The nightclub was on the second floor. Pablo Váldes and his band were playing at 11. With the 10 CUC entrance fee, you could order drinks and food deducted from it. The big posh room had tables along the windows facing the sea. The bar was to the left and the stage at the far end. The show still an hour away, there was no more than a dozen customers. I sat down at one of the tables in front of the stage. I ordered a beer to start and penne arrabbiata for dinner.

Escorted by a Cuban, two American blondes in their 30's sat down in the adjacent table. The beer came and I lit a cigarette. A few puffs into it, the Cuban leaned over and said, "Would you mind putting out the cigarette? It is bothering the ladies." If there is one freedom guaranteed to Cubans, it is the liberty to smoke anywhere and I was damned if I was going to let the Smoking Gestapo of the States reach me in Cuba of all places and encumber my nasty habit.

"Please tell the ladies they're bothering *me* with their request. Besides, I was sitting here first. If the smoke bothers them, they can sit somewhere else." The man shrugged his shoulders and translated my message to the women. The nearest one looked at me, insulted. I blew a cloud, she blew at the cloud in a huff, stood up and the others followed her to another table. "Thank you," I said in English.

The arrabbiata arrived and sure enough it was the worst ever, with a bland, tasteless tomato sauce without the fire and spice that usually accompanies it. Instead of penne, it was overcooked spaghetti. They say that hunger is the best sauce and that was the only condiment in this dish. I began to wonder when I was going to eat a good meal in Cuba. As 11 neared, the room filled; almost everyone was a foreigner save for the Cubans on some tourist's payroll as escorts or guides. I couldn't imagine the average Cuban spending nearly a month's salary on one night at a club. But when the band struck up and the elegance of Cuban jazz fluttered the air, it crossed my mind that it might just be worth it, at least just once. For 90 minutes, the 12-member band enraptured its audience. The bad food in no way lessened my enjoyment of the band.

After the band left the stage and many were filing out, I decided to have a nightcap at the bar where a cordial young bartender served me a mojito. I asked him if he knew how much the musicians made per night.

"All licensed musicians make 7 CUC per night."

"No matter what?"

"No matter what."

"Now that sounds like a good deal."

"That's right. Musicians can't complain. The state takes really good care of them."

"And rightly so. What I heard tonight was the spirit of this nation and it was beautiful."

"Thank you, sir," he said as I stood up and passed him the money for the drink.

"Keep the change."

"Thank you. By the way, if you don't mind my asking, where are you from, sir?"

"I'm from here. Goodnight."

Cuban music: Most of what people all over the world consider Latin music, originated in Cuba. With its no less than 20 genres and rhythms that mix African, Spanish-Arab, and American jazz forms, its breadth and influence are the most extensive of all the musical traditions that emerged after the conquest of Latin America. The only traditions that even approach it as rivals are Mexican and Brazilian music. There's nothing over the top in Cuban music. It is imbued with a grace and complexity of syncopation, rhythm and harmony seldom found in any other music, except for jazz. But it offers something that cerebral jazz does not: a sassy insouciance that can only come from the mixture of Spanish arrogance and blithe African physicality.

Poised as the first ports of call between the Americas, the two largest cities, La Havana in the west and Santiago de Cuba in the east, Cuban music blossomed at these cities from 500 years of cultural exchange. Cubans adapted musical traditions from many countries and blended them with their own to create one of the world's greatest musical traditions. It was once world-popular when Xavier Cugat and Ricky Ricardo gave the big band era extra legs before rock and roll took over. In the taxi back to the guesthouse, I reflected on what the bartender had said and how the regime had affected Cuban music. After the revolution, almost all casinos, cabarets and nightclubs were closed, eliminating work for most musicians. As is typical in communist states, an emphasis on classical performing arts evolved, coupled with a rejection of popular music, especially rock and roll. There is no question the arts and especially music benefit from cultural exchange, not from isolation (jazz, flamenco, Cuban, Mexican and Brazilian music, all blends of many musical traditions are the most salient examples). This and the virtual disappearance of tourism from the island (until the fall of the Soviet Union forced Fidel to reconsider) arrested the development of Cuban music. Instead, it was advanced elsewhere. Salsa, a blend of several Cuban musical genres, was developed in New York City in the 60's and 70's for the most part by Puerto Rican Americans. There is no question, however, that the regime has promoted excellent musicianship with its free education programs and its special preference for the role of musicians, particularly after tourism was again promoted after the early 90's.

Now on the way home in the taxi along the Malecón, all I could hear from the festive crowd was hip-hop and reggaeton. I knew that these foreign imports would be sooner or later adapted and transformed into something beautiful and Cuban.

Then something struck me that snapped me out of my musings about music. It was past one in the morning and the Malecón for miles teemed with people partying before the ocean. In fact, there may have been a stadium full of people engaged in all the imaginable rituals of leisure out along the promenade as we sped past. I asked the driver why so many people gathered here.

"Lots of reasons. To escape the heat, socialize, party, sex."

"So they bring their own drinks and party away, is that it?"

"That's about it."

"But the volume of people is what gets me. I mean there might be 60,000 people out there now."

"Ah, it's that most can't afford any other place to party. So they get a bottle of rum between three or four people, a soda bottle and you got yourself a party. Cheap. Rum is cheap in Cuba."

"How much is a cheap bottle?"

"You can get one for like two CUC."

This reminded me of reading long ago how the common folk made a party in the old Soviet Union and the Eastern Bloc. Three people, a bottle of vodka, and a kitchen. That's all they needed. But then again, that's about all they had.

That night leaning back on the pillow thinking about the last thing the driver with the pod-like car had said, "You wouldn't believe how much stealing from the government goes on, corruption. It's all crap," I came to the conclusion that it was necessarily so, for when the legal means for a decent life don't work, people will turn to illegal means. Eli, the *bicitaxista* I was soon to meet, would tell me that the black market is the real economy; he'd also tell me almost everyone is in on it. Because nearly everything is stolen and no initial capital is invested for the product, it tends to be very cheap. But unlike black markets in other countries, which deal mostly with illegal products like drugs or weapons, the Cuban market deals with everything under the sun, from diapers to toilet paper to soap and toothpaste, reflecting the failure of the regime in supplying the people's most elementary needs. The people of Cuba have developed one of those attitudes similar to that of music sharing in the West. Although it is stealing, nobody thinks about it that way— if they even think about it at all. It is said that half of Cuba is connected to the black market and the other half is its customer. One driver later told me that, "Since everything belongs to the government and the government keeps saying that everything it has is for the people, the people don't see anything wrong with taking what's already theirs a little early."

In Cuba reign supreme some of the worst sins of Latin American countries: nepotism, corruption, disdain for the rule of law, graft and apathy. If only Che Guevara, the first architect of Cuba's communism, had been a little wiser, less of an idealist and more a pragmatist, it might have been a real revolution. But because the ideal was forced on the real, Cuba was turned into a polite fiction, a dollar-a-day Worker's Paradise, a "Giving Tree" with all the rotten yet intact roots of the Spanish Empire.

DAY THREE

The plan was to take care of my birth certificate problem. First I had to go to the Ministry of External Affairs, which I'd learned was in El Vedado. It was in this neighborhood that my family had spent its last days in Cuba before exile. I walked to the Malecón Boulevard to get a *colectivo*. On the walk, that tug of nostalgia hit me hard again and I wandered back to those days when my family had its struggle to be free...

We had begun to prepare to flee to the States. I remember that during part of my childhood in Cuba, there was a time I was not quite sure my father was in complete control of his faculties. For years, he'd spent an hour each night at his desk talking to himself in a strange language I later learned was English. Now he stepped up his studies and I would hear him hour after hour carefully preparing and enacting conversations on all topics between himself and his American alter-ego, an invisible man he called "Mr. Faycund." He tried to sell our house in Holguín and others on mother's side of the family, but there were no buyers since everyone by now knew that private property was going the way of the dodo. Unable to sell the houses, their keys were left with friends and relatives, who all eventually had to relinquish them to the state. It seemed everything we owned now had little value or was a burden to our plan of flight as our world was being dismantled by remote, unseen forces. Mother began to sell or give away furniture and household goods. Father managed to sell the 1956 Chevrolet Bel Air to four men who drove it away one day. With this money and the little he was able to rescue before his accounts were frozen, we packed all we had left in the world in six suitcases and left on a bus for Havana.

We moved into a guest house in El Vedado. In the colonial era, it had belonged to a Spanish aristocrat, but now it housed about 30 guests and served them three meals a day included in the price of the rooms. This would be our home while we waited for a visa from our own government to exit our own country. That by now we lived in a totalitarian state was an open secret. The government controlled every aspect of daily life—from what one was able to say to what one was able to eat to what one's children were able to learn in school. Food was now rationed and all selection and choice of goods had disappeared. I remember dining on only spaghetti with tomato sauce and rice for a month before some canned meat from Czechoslovakia finally arrived. Because toilet paper disappeared now and then, we were forced to use newspaper that we crumbled and splayed until it softened. In the meantime, our parents had decided not to let us go to school because they knew the children were having their brains cooked in communist ideology. Instead, Consuelo did her best to teach us at home. One after-

El Vedado, the former upper-middle-class Havana district where my family stayed waiting "for a visa from our own government to exit our own country." Its name means "the forbidden" since in the days of the real "Pirates of the Caribbean" the local *caudillo* forbid any road or path development in the area to prevent the pirates' access to the then walled city of Havana, today called La Habana Vieja, or Old Havana.

noon I was playing in the garden that faced the street. Some children my age walking home after school saw me there out of uniform and started screaming *Imperialista! Capitalista!*. My father, who had heard them from the veranda, called in a loud whisper, "Gabriel, come inside! Didn't I tell you not to go in the garden at this hour?" Years later, I would wonder how such words could come out of the mouths of children.

I flagged down a '58 Oldsmobile *colectivo* on the Malecón Boulevard and got in with five citizens already in it. I told the driver I'd heard the ministry was not far off between Calle Linea and the Malecón Boulevard. "*Tranquilo*," he said, "I'll drop you off at the cross street." About 8 blocks later he pulled over and said, "The ministry is to the right about three blocks down this street." I thanked him and he nodded like so many Cubans are wont to do, with a slow lowering and opening of his eyes. I gave him about twice the fare and told him to keep the change. Again the nod with the eyes and he was off on his route back and forth along Malecón Boulevard, trailing a wake of fumes.

The ministry was down a broad avenue of hotels that led from the Malecón. It was a multistory corner building that itself had been a hotel before the Revolution. I walked into the empty lobby where a big black man sat reading a magazine, his legs propped up on the desk in front. He removed his eyes from the magazine and looked up at me. "May I help you?" His eyes were dead and bored as he scrutinized me as if I were a giant lobster he was checking for freshness.

"Yes, I understand I need to have my birth certificate authenticated by this ministry before presenting it to the Costa Rican Embassy." He didn't say a word; instead he opened a drawer and produced a form and began writing on it. Then he said, "Identification?" I handed him my passport. He opened it and began copying its information on the form. When finished he put the form inside the passport and shoved it toward me, eyes down.

"Take this document to the address on it." I looked at the paper and saw that it was a lawyer's office in Miramar.

"You mean the authentication isn't done here?"

"You got it."

"You are so kind. I commend you on your alacrity, really."

The lawyer's office in Miramar was posh by Cuban standards and so was the service. I didn't have to wait long to be attended to by a beautiful woman lawyer who had me sign a contract in order to authenticate the birth certificate and have it sent to the Costa Rican embassy for the certification which cost almost a year's salary for the average Cuban.

"That's a year's salary for the average Cuban," I said after signing.

"But then you're not the average Cuban," she said, batting her eyelashes with a radiant smile.

"But I am in Cuba. What do you charge the average Cuban for this service, a service that in the United States would cost $5?"

"The average Cuban doesn't need this service."

"What if he did?"

"We would probably charge two CUC's."

"I hope you see a certain irony in that in the U.S., that is about what they'd charge to *anyone* no matter what his nationality. Isn't that what's called discrimination?"

"Again, you're not Cuban, but North American."

"Actually I am Cuban; as you can see in the passport, I was born here."

"Your passport is North American, therefore, so are you." The smile still radiant.

"So are you."

"So am I what?"

"You are also North American."

"I don't understand." A frown replaced the smile.

"I'm surprised you don't know that every country from Panama northward, including the Caribbean, is part of the North American Continent," I said smiling, "so you're North American."

"I see where you're going," her smile returning, "It's just that you North Americans, calling yourselves Americans, have expropriated for yourselves the name of America. I am an American, we're all Americans; so why should you alone call yourselves Americans?"

"We 'Americans' don't deny you the right to call yourself an American. But it just so happens that language is full of words that mean more than one thing. So why can't an American be both a citizen of the United States and the Americas?"

"Because then we can't tell what you refer to when you say you're 'Americans.' You could be from any country in this hemisphere."

"Now you're pretending that you wouldn't know what I meant if I said, 'I'm an American.' Besides, let me ask you, what do you call Canadians?"

"Canadians."

"They're not North Americans?"

"They're also North Americans."

"So you see, a North American can mean both a citizen of Canada and of the U.S. One word, two meanings. But in reality you'd never call a Canadian a North American would you?"

"No, not normally."

"Why not?"

"Well, I guess because we wouldn't know which country in North America they'd be from."

"Precisely. So if you call a U.S. citizen a North American, you would also not know which country in North America he'd be from."

"In theory, but in practice everyone knows that you're referring only to an American."

"Sorry, but didn't you mean a North American."

"Now you're making my head spin with all these semantics. Yes, I meant a North American."

"So let's turn your argument around. Don't you think the Canadians, or Mexicans for that matter, should resent the fact that *you* and many in Latin America have expropriated the name of North America to refer only to the citizens of the United States? What about Cubans? Cubans are North Americans too, yet you have expropriated the name of North America to mean only citizens of the U.S. Maybe *you* should feel a little resentment."

"We might if you North Americans had treated us better."

"Touché, Miss..." I looked at her nameplate. "Miss Hurtado; now we're getting to the bottom of things. And you have a point. The U.S. has not treated Latin America well and it shows. The resentment is so deep that you ignore logic and reason even when just referring to Americans."

"Touché. You realize that human beings are not just made of reason and logic."

"I like you."

"I like you too."

"I'd like to invite you to dinner."

"I'm busy and married. But thank you."

"As usual I'm too late."

"No hurry. You still have spark."

"Thanks. How long is this going to take? "

"The certification? About two or three weeks."

"Two or three weeks? Any way that can be hurried? My plane leaves next week Saturday. Why so long?"

"Well, we have to send it to the Costa Rican embassy, then they have to certify it and send it back to us, then we send it to the Ministry of External Affairs and they return it to us. You pick it up here. I'll see what I can do about hurrying this for you; here's my card."

I walked back to a nearby taxi stop where they served lunch at a streetside café. I ordered a Cristal and a sandwich. The beer was good and refreshing, but the sandwich, another disaster. Then I took a taxi back to Casa Nilma. Asked the inevitable question on the way, the driver delivered himself of the usual complaints before he added, "By the way, are you sure you're not being followed?"

"As a matter of fact, no. I got that impression this morning when I turned around and saw a guy look away about 20 meters behind me."

"Watch yourself and what you say in public. These bastards don't fool around."

I thanked him for the advice and he continued with his gripes. Listening to his lamentations, my mind returned to the conversation with the lawyer. The obsession (which picked up steam with the advent of the Cuban Revolution; before the Revolution almost everyone referred to Americans as Americans) of all Latin countries in refusing to call Americans by their adopted name is indeed illogical and grounded in sheer emotional resentment. The U.S. is the only country in the world whose citizens are not referred to by the name they call themselves. An entire continent, including Spain and Portugal, its colonial conquerors, has adopted this custom. The underlying notion is that "they think they are usurping the names American and America for themselves," which is in line with their historical treatment and perception of Latin America as "their own back yard." Indeed, the United States has been no angel and has managed to behave in exactly the way the Castro brothers portrayed it to behave toward its Latin neighbors. Here is a list of the most notable interventions by which they have played into the Castros' hand:

1898: The U.S. declares war on Spain, blaming it for the *Maine* explosion and enabling it to usurp Cuba's war of independence.

1910: U.S. Marines occupy Nicaragua to help support their man, Adolfo Díaz.

1915: U.S. Marines occupy Haiti to restore order, establishing a protectorate until 1934.

1916: Marines occupy Dominican Republic, stay until 1924.

1926: The U.S. tried to occupy Nicaragua, but General Augusto Sandino began an armed resistance that culminated in the abandonment of the country by the U.S. because the Great Depression and Sandino's success made it a losing proposition.

1954: The CIA overthrew Guatemala's elected Jacob Arbenz in a military coup. Arbenz had threatened to nationalize the Rockefeller-owned United Fruit Company, in which CIA Director Allen Dulles also owned stock; he was replaced by a series of right-wing dictators whose bloodthirsty policies would kill thousands in the next 40 years.

1959: The U.S. military helped "Papa Doc" Duvalier become dictator of Haiti. He created his own private police force, the "Tonton Macoutes," who terrorized the population. Thousands would die during the Duvalier family reign. The U.S. never protested their dismal human rights record.

1961: The CIA-backed military forced the democratically elected president of Ecuador, José Velasco, to resign. The CIA engineered the Bay of Pigs invasion of Cuba by 1,500 Cuban expatriates.

1964: A CIA-backed military coup overthrew Brazil's democratically elected government of João Goulart. The military junta that replaced him turned out to be one of the most oppressive and bloodthirsty in Latin American history.

1965: A popular rebellion broke out in the Dominican Republic, aiming to reinstall Juan Bosch as the country's elected leader. The revolution was crushed when U.S. Marines landed to uphold the military regime.

1973: The CIA orchestrated the overthrow and murder in Chile of Salvador Allende, Latin America's first elected socialist leader.

1976: The CIA helped in the establishment of the military dictatorship of Argentina.

1980: The U.S. began its meddling in the Salvadoran conflict.
1983: Grenada was invaded.
1989: Panama was invaded.[1]

That the majority of these illegal interventions were done in the spirit of fighting communism hardly exonerates America (and it must be asserted that as often as not it was motivated also by self-interest or by service to the profit motive). Humanity has traditionally mitigated guilt by applying the two great resorts with which it has suspended the black-and-whiteness of morality: "the lesser of two evils" and "the end justifies the means."

Jeanne Kirkpatrick, the former American ambassador to the UN, voiced such justifications, which came to be called "The Kirkpatrick Doctrine." It was based on a simple premise: Authoritarian dictatorships tend to be inherently unstable and tend to endure only as long as the dictator remains in power. Communist dictatorships, on the other hand, are more stable because a transcendent ideology cements them and because they are totalitarian by nature, controlling every aspect of a society. (One need only look at the two last bastions of pure totalitarian communism, whose continuity has been achieved through the familial inheritance of power: Cuba and North Korea.) Therefore, if one must choose between them, with the hope that democracy would result in the long run, it is better to support an authoritarian dictatorship.

A key consideration also played a role during the Cold War: If a country fell into the grip of communism, its sovereignty was guaranteed by the Soviet Union, and the Soviets had nuclear teeth, making transition to democracy even more unlikely.[2]

Historical events seem to confirm America's adherence to the doctrine. The last U.S. military intervention in Latin America, the invasion of Panama, coincided with the fall of the Soviet Union in 1989. Since then, and in spite of the many leftist regimes that have cropped up in Latin America—Bolivia, Nicaragua, Venezuela, Ecuador, Argentina—the U.S. has done nothing resembling the "old days." Regardless of the motives and sincerity behind the U.S. policy, its interventions have not helped its cause to win the hearts of Latin Americans, who by and large have little comprehension of geopolitical maneuvers. Today, in all the aforementioned countries, the elected leftist regimes have run on anti–American, "anti-imperialist" tickets and they never cease to remind their constituents of the former American abuse of power.

Arriving at Casa Nilma, the mouth-watering smell of roasting pork rushed at me as I opened the door. Nilma was in the kitchen, busy preparing the feast with Yendri, the wife of Ramón the taxi driver. Yendri was a plump woman with a special light in her eyes, a mixture of innocence and temptation. She was what some men might call "a dumpling." I instantly liked her. I exclaimed, "Nilma, I'm salivating like one of Pavlov's dogs! And I didn't even need the bell!" The ladies laughed and welcomed me. They showed me the roasting piglet in the oven, which caused a rumble in my stomach that the ladies heard, setting off their laughter again.

Nilma then said to me, "I had a little problem today when I went to report your stay to immigration. In your visa under nationality it says: Cuban-American. They didn't like that; they want you to declare that you're either one or the other, not both. So which one do you want to claim?"

"Your roast piglet has reminded me that I'm first a Cuban; so let's say that."

"Fine, I'll do so. Also, just for your information, they also wanted to know what you were doing here, so I told them about your birth certificate. And they wanted to know my impression of you, so I told them that you seemed well-educated, a gentleman."

"I appreciate your standing up for me, Nilma, thank you. But I find this unusual. Do they question you so about every guest?"

"No, you're the first one, but then you're the first Cuban-American I ever had here, so please be advised," she leaned forward and whispered, "they get into everything here." Then she took me aside as Yendri busied herself in the kitchen. "Now let me tell you, tonight my brother, Jaime, is coming to dinner. He's a writer for the *Granma*, you know, the official state newspaper. He's a good man, but a real communist. Just to let you know."

This intimation took me back a bit, for it meant that Nilma understood what my political beliefs might be and that she wanted to protect me from any consequences resulting from political discussions that might crop up that night. "Thanks for telling me, Nilma," I said. "I'll keep it in mind. Listen, what do you think the majority of the guests would like to drink tonight? I'm going out around the Capitol and on the way back I can stop at a liquor store."

"That's easy; beer is everyone's favorite."

I went out following Juanito's map to the Parque Central. The boat *Granma* was housed, much like Lenin's corpse in the old Soviet Union, inside a glass mausoleum in the middle of a wooded square. There was a soldier at each corner of the mausoleum. One gave me the wary eye as I used the zoom to take photos. I left the square and walked toward El Capitolio. Looking at the colonial architecture I remembered reading that Castro had abandoned the maintenance of the capital in order to concentrate on developing the countryside. Now I saw the result of that neglect. Havana used to be called "The Pearl of the Caribbean," "The Paris of the Americas." It was a white city with pastel colors intermittently relieving the whiteness. A beautiful, bustling city. Today most of Old Havana is grimy gray. In 1982, UNESCO declared Old Havana a World Heritage Site and allocated funds to its reconstruction and preservation. In this and other strolls, I saw little evidence that this money had been put to work. Save for the restoration to Calle Obispo, the buildings around the Parque Central and La Plaza Vieja, squalid dilapidated buildings line the narrow streets. Only the most monumental buildings considered tourist attractions have been reconstructed. Buttresses often prop up floors and balconies. Many old façades have scaffolding around them that have turned into the framework supporting walls of crawling vines. Once as I walked along Calle Obispo, I looked in the windows of many buildings and saw gutted interiors: only the façades had been restored. Then there are *los derrumbes*. Once in a while most citizens of Havana hear a *cataplum!*, the onomatopoeia for a *derrumbe*, a collapsing building that takes the life of whoever is in it. *Derrumbes* officially don't exist, but everyone knows they do because of what they call *la radio bemba* or the lip radio.

What is refreshing about Havana is what it doesn't have: neon, glitz, and ubiquitous advertisement (except, of course, T-shirt ads, which international marketing has somehow convinced people that the vulgarity of turning themselves into free ambulating billboards is hip). Absent are the over-the-top flash of Vegas, the sterility of Main Street,

USA, and the bombardment of noise and neon of Hong Kong, Tokyo or Bangkok. Instead, it has the feel of a tropical version of the old quarters of European cities, where they have prohibited neon and limited advertisement to preserve the ancient ambiance. Add to this the vintage American cars and one feels the aura of a place where time has stood still. More by unintended circumstance than by design, Havana is a curious anachronism, for capitalism is officially illegal and, therefore, most advertisement is of the Revolution and its heroes. On billboards, murals, and statues always in half profile, Lenin, Marx, Camilo Cienfuegos, and especially El Che, eyes, looking somewhere up and off to the left, constantly pierce a visionary future. Havana, nevertheless, has its own quirky charm and vivaciousness thanks to the curious blend of soviet austerity and the grace and spontaneity of the people.

I came around a corner and suddenly before me loomed El Capitolio with the Parque Central around it. This stately capitol, modeled after the one in Washington, like many buildings was closed for remodeling it into a museum. I photographed it and the surrounding buildings then sat at a bench for a rest. I looked toward Chinatown's gate where a soldier stood guard with a German shepherd on a leash that led off his Kalashnikov. Standing up, I pointed the zoom right at him as he glared poison at me through an angry frown. Click. Click. Click. He didn't like it, but then, I couldn't care less. After taking some shots of passersby for a while, an old man in a baseball cap and a threadbare navy blue blazer walked up to me and said in English, "Where djou from?"

"From the United States," said I in Spanish to make it easier for him.

Switching to Spanish he said, "Your accent is very good. How did you learn to speak so well?"

"Well, I was born here but raised in the States. I left Cuba when I was a boy."

"Ah, really? Do you mind if I sit down?"

"Not at all. Please sit."

He sat and we traded small talk for a while, then he asked, "What do you think of Cuba now?"

Since I didn't know his political bent I said, "Well, it looks poorer than when I was a boy. There was more activity and Havana was cleaner, not so run down looking as now. But you must remember this; you were a young man when I was a boy."

He bowed his head and thought for a moment then looked up at me again, his eyes' sagged lower lids exposing the pink insides. "Yes, I remember. I think I can talk to you honestly."

"Please do; don't worry. I'm really not from here."

"I'm too old to worry. What can they do to me now that time has not already done?" I didn't answer. "I'm an old man on his last legs, so what do they even care?"

"They?" I pretended.

"You know *they*, the regime. Look at me. I fought in Angola, was wounded, came back, and was a civil servant. I gave my life to them, most of it anyway, but a while ago I just started pretending. This was when I realized my whole life had been wasted. Look at me... And you must excuse me because I drank a little rum just before I met you... But here I am, nearly 82 years old and all I have is a garret and a 10 dollar-a-month pension after a lifetime of service and devotion to these sons of whores."

"I'm so sorry. This is one of the reasons my family left. I know this isn't exactly a place where you can fulfill your dreams."

"Dreams? You can have *their* dreams, not your own. Everything has to go through *them*. Then whatever's left, what they let you have, is yours. But look at me. What you see before you is what they let me have."

I noticed that in spite of his assurances that he didn't care what happened to him, his eyes still darted around behind me. "You're still afraid, aren't you? Don't *they* like what you're doing now?"

"Maybe it's an old habit. But yes, they don't like it when we talk too long with foreigners, especially like this, one to one. They assume we're learning of how it really is outside, which doesn't help their cause."

"So I see nothing has changed. My uncle spent eight years in prison just on suspicion and he really was doing nothing against them."

"Like him, so many. They have all the power." I got up to say good-bye and told him it had been good for me to talk to him and thanked him for his honesty. He stood up and walked a little with me and said, "I'll never see you again, but somehow it has made me feel better to talk to you, even though all we talked about was unpleasant and probably a waste of time. Now shake hands with an old man to whom you brought some relief."

I shook his hand and said, "Nothing like what you told me is a waste. I will tell others back home and in some small way it may help bring some change. Take care of yourself." I walked away and for some reason I looked back and there he was still standing where I left him, still looking at me walking away. I waved and he waved back, an old man with nothing except bitter memories and what I had just given him, an ear to his wounded heart. It struck me as I walked that almost every Cuban I had thus far talked to privately had used me as a vent for frustration.

As I walked home along the gardens surrounding the Capitolio, a mulatto about my age pedaled up to me in one of Havana's ubiquitous *bicitaxis*, a tricycle with a canopy and a seat for two over the back wheels. He offered to take me home for a CUC.

I asked, "How do you know I don't live 10 kilometers away?"

"I don't care, I'll still take you." I thought to myself: "Now that's a hell of a sales pitch. How can one say no?"

"I bet you're counting on the kindness of my heart if it's too far."

"No, I saw you were walking home, so figured it can't be far."

"How can I say no?"

"You can't." I got in. After he was sure of whom he was conversing with, Eli was opening up to me about the misery of life in Cuba. We were pedaling past an austere three-story building with bars on all the windows and he said, "It doesn't take much to land you in there. Suspicion is enough. See that woman in there?" I glanced to the left to see a girl through the bars sitting on a cot. "She's waiting to be interrogated. "Have you eaten the food here?" he said, changing the topic. I told him of my wretched introduction. He continued, "I know what good food is because I can remember it when I was a boy. But I'll tell you a modern Cuban joke: "In Cuba we have three good things and three bad things. The three good things are education, health care and sports. The three bad things are breakfast, lunch and dinner!" I had to laugh at this typically clever Cuban humor. Then I asked, "Do you know any good restaurants?"

"There's not many, but I know of one not far from here and they have a great flamenco show to boot; it's called El Guajirito." Just then we were pulling up to the Casa Nilma. "If you like I can pick you up later and take you there."

"Not tonight, I have a dinner to attend. But how about tomorrow at eight?"

"Good. I'll be here at eight tomorrow." We parted and I went to a nearby liquor shop to buy a case of Cristal for the party. At the shop it cost 1 CUC per unit or 24 CUC for the case. Now I understood why Nilma had immediately said that beer was everyone's favorite: Cubans can't afford to drink their own beer since a six-pack costs almost half a month's wage.

The case cuddled in my arms, the guests, who had already arrived, welcomed me. Yendri came up, offered her cheek to be kissed and took the case away while Nilma introduced me to those I hadn't met. There was Tomás, Ana's fifty-something boyfriend, already a little tipsy from the rum on the rocks he was holding. Then I met Isabel, the lovely young lady who had handled my reservation by e-mail, Carolina, Nilma's childhood friend from Beirut, and finally, Jaime, Nilma's brother, the *Granma* writer, who had a strong resemblance to Vyacheslav Molotov. He greeted me with a wary perfunctory politeness. I couldn't help noticing that he was by far the best dressed Cuban I had thus far met—a salmon pink linen *guayabera*, black trousers with good drape, and patent leather shoes.

The scent of roasting pork saturated the apartment. Ana came and handed out beers and while she and Yendri prepared things in the kitchen, the rest of the party gravitated to the balcony to watch the sun set over Havana Bay. Deferring by tacit agreement the divan to Carolina, Nilma and Isabel, Jaime, Tomás and I stood or leaned against the railing. We toasted to Carolina's return from Beirut. The gold of the setting sun against the women's faces, I asked them to pose for a shot. My suggestion stirred the women into a preening frenzy; then they struck poses well rehearsed. When I showed the ladies the photo, their faces ardent in the autumnal light, the last vestiges of insecurity faded and the mood turned toward informality. The conversation fell on my background. I explained simply that my family had left in 1962 and that I had returned to get my birth certificate. I was never asked about life in the States, as if they knew all about it already or they weren't interested or they were afraid to broach the subject. Noticing that the conversation might head to an impasse, I asked Carolina about life in Beirut.

"Oh, it's truly a good life. The people are so warm and the climate, wonderful."

"Yes, and Lebanese food is considered the best in the Arab world."

"Exactly! Have you been to the Middle East? Not many Westerners know this."

"Yes, I taught at university in Saudi Arabia, so I know very well how Lebanese cuisine is regarded in that region. But how about the revolution in Syria? Isn't that affecting you in any way?"

"Of course, we're getting more and more refugees," said Carolina, "and it's putting a strain on everything."

Testing the waters in an area away from Cuba, I ventured forth: "But at least the people are finally toppling dictators in Arab countries. The so-called Arab Spring. That has to be good, don't you think?"

"Oh, be careful," retorted Carolina. "I don't trust the Moslem Brotherhood and where they're going."

"I couldn't agree with you more. But you know it's inspiring to see these long suppressed people rise up against the yoke of dictators: Tunisia, Libya, Egypt, now Syria. For the first time in the history of the region, it is the government that fears the people and not the other way around. This is the key to a healthy society. The people should not fear the government. The government should fear the people."

It was as if I had dropped a bomb on the conversation. Everyone's eyes darted askance and no one said a word. What I had said was an inevitable conclusion that perhaps had never occurred to anyone present, yet its logic and portent for their own lives was as incontrovertible as it was unacceptable. Everyone in Cuba fears the government, even those who support it, for they know the consequences of stepping out of bounds. I had created a great internal commotion in all present. The Cuban Revolution had supplanted a government its people feared. Yet now, friend or foe, everyone fears the Revolution.

Mercifully, Yendri came and sang out, "Dinner is served!"

We all filed into the living-dining room and beheld the table. The piglet roast lay golden brown like a planet surrounded in the grip of its gravity by satellites of rice, black beans, fried plantain, tossed salad, yucca, fried vegetables and bread. It was a spread fit for kings and compliments poured forth from all. I was to have my first decent meal in Cuba. I was ushered for some reason to the seat at one of the heads of the table as if I were a guest of honor. Molotov, who from time to time would give me a wary look, occupied the other head. Beers popped open for Nilma's toast to friendship and good company. We clinked glasses, drank and descended on the feast. As always with good food, the conversation disappeared while everyone had the first bite. Following the compliments to the chefs, Nilma, Yendri and Ana, the unpleasant direction of the conversation I had caused turned to the wonders of various Cuban dishes. But it would not last. Yendri asked me about my visit to the Jazz Café. I had nothing but good things to say about the music, but then she asked, "Did you have dinner there?"

"Yes, I did." But she pressed on.

"Did you like it?"

"Actually, it was terrible, which surprised me in a way, but not in another."

"What do you mean?"

"Well, it surprised me considering the nightclub's class, but then it didn't surprise me in that this here is the first good meal I've had since arriving in Cuba."

"You can thank the North American embargo for that!" said Jaime, who had been listening.

"Really? How so, Don Jaime?" I asked, knowing full well that the honorific "don" is viewed in Cuba as a vestige of the old colonial days.

"Because of the embargo we have shortages of many things, including spices and many basic needs for cooking."

I looked at him and realized from the set of his jaw he was in for a fight. A voice just then inside me said, "What the hell. Go for it."

"Well," I said, picking up my glass of beer, "You certainly seem to have enough beer and rum, thank God!"

"That's because we make it ourselves. Otherwise, we would have shortages of that too."

"Now, Don Jaime, when I was a boy here, my family had a farm and I distinctly remember this garden we had behind the house where we grew everything for the kitchen, from spices to vegetables to fruit. I also remember our meals were delicious and lacked nothing for their preparation. So you're telling me that in today's Cuba, you can't grow your own spices and vegetables?"

"We can and we do! But we lack the farm machinery for mass harvest that the Yankees don't let us have. They choke our people with that embargo!"

"Correct me if I'm wrong, Don Jaime, but the embargo doesn't seem to prevent Cuban products from populating the shelves of every country I've been in except the United States. This means that you trade with all these countries, from Japan to Spain to Costa Rica, where I live now. I also know that the United States isn't the only country that manufactures farm machinery. I'm sure you can get them from Europe or Brazil or at least the old Eastern Bloc. Now tell me, aren't you exaggerating a bit the influence of the embargo? After all, you seem to have all the machinery for mass producing beer." I looked at my glass of Cristal.

Jaime turned communist red. "No, no, no. You have it all wrong…" Just then Nilma put her hand on his arm and said, "Come now, *compañeros*, let's stop this talk of politics! Before you know it you'll get indigestion and ruin this wonderful meal."

"You're right, Nilma, I agree! Don Jaime, let's toast to the chefs!" No one could disagree and even Jaime seemed a little relieved, for I suspected this was the first time in a long time, maybe never, that anyone had challenged his words and forced him to think outside the dark little box of the party line. We all raised our glasses and the rest of the evening was spent in amicable chatter interlaced with the occasional glower I caught from Jaime.

That night I went to bed reflecting on the conversation with Jaime and on Jaime himself. I thought about the fifty-year-old U.S. embargo and the sheer idiocy of it all. Not only has it not succeeded in dethroning the regime, it has only helped to strengthen it. Of course, the embargo does hurt the Cuban economy, but it does so more from missed opportunity than from actual direct harm. There is no question that not being able to trade with the world's largest and richest market represents a huge loss. But the overwhelming problem with the Cuban economy is the Cuban economy. The proof is in the pudding of the current state of Venezuela. It also functions with a command economy and the results have been the familiar ones—lack of basic products, long lines to buy anything, diminished buying power for the people and a host of other problems. Yet the Castro brothers to this day milk the old embargo for every political gain they can squeeze from its udders, blaming it for all their failures and those of the absurd, chimerical economy they created. Jaime's denunciation of the embargo reflected the familiar posture. The shortages of the most basic goods and the long lines to acquire them are not due to the topsy-turvy nature of a command economy, wherein prices are set by committee, no one knows the real demand, and the supply is determined by educated guesses; it's the embargo. That there are only 300,000 cars in a country of 11 million people is not caused by the fact that no one can buy a car, or anything of any value, on a 15 to 20 dollar salary; it's the embargo. In fact, the party line explanation for the adoption of the *libreta*, or system of monthly rations, was that the government was forced to feed the people on account of, you guessed it, the embargo. Meanwhile, the embargo engenders sympathy for the regime and vilification for the Americans. The UN General Assembly gives the U.S. its annual black eye by voting almost unanimously to rescind the embargo, the only naysayers being the Americans, the Israelis and the Marshall Islanders.

Jaime: I pondered on what kind of a writer would be content with dedicating his life to an endless series of lies, half-truths, or omissions of the truth. Writers and artists seek the truth. It's their mantra. Journalists by their professional nature aim at the exposure of the facts. So how is it that Jaime could have submerged all that for the benefit of the regime?

I guessed he was in his mid-fifties, which means he was born a little after the Revolution's triumph in 1959. He never had a chance. They took him from the cradle and molded him like you mold a clay vase off a potter's wheel. He was never told about the Society of Professional Journalists Code of Ethics' Four Principles: Seek and report the truth. Minimize harm. Act independently. Be accountable and transparent.[3]

The regime drilled into him that communism is the one true ideology and that he shall have no others before it. They warned him of speaking, and even thinking, against the only true ideology and that all others were false and evil and corrupt. They limited contact with the outside world through the regime's prohibition of foreign travel as well as through the usual obstacles to the access of information. Jaime never learned any arguments against their ideology, only those in support of it and only its arguments against all other ideologies. He read only the books they chose for him to read, but he never had a choice anyway since no other books besides those that favored their ideology existed. They rewarded him with medals and certificates at each good showing along the way to make sure he felt a good boy. They rendered unto him only the ideas and thoughts that they wanted to float about his brain. In brief, the regime had nearly lobotomized his intellect through the obstruction of input and the desecration of the truth. Before fading to sleep, I decided that Jaime was not only innocent but also, in a deviant way, *an* innocent.

DAY FOUR

The following day I made it a point to go to a nearby bar to pick up a *Granma* copy just to see what it was like these days. I walked in and in an audible voice for most of the clientele said to the barkeep, "I understand you sell the *Granma* here."

The bartender went to a stack in the corner, came back and said, "20 *centavos.*"

"Great," I said, "Now I can really get to the truth about the world." This utterance caused snorts and chuckles in the clientele as I walked out smiling.

I leaned against a corner building and looked it over: eight pages in broadsheet format. The title *Granma* was in a red cursive at the top, on its right, a black and white photo of Fidel and Raúl along with their fellow rebels in the background thrusting their rifles at the sky in triumph. The top left corner showed the date, edition number, and then a little message: *La Habana, Año 54 de la Revolución* (Havana, Year 54 of the Revolution). Beneath this was the subtitle: *ÓRGANO OFICIAL DEL COMITÉ CENTRAL DEL PARTIDO COMUNISTA DE CUBA* (Official Organ of the Central Committee of the Cuban Communist Party). The main headline, also in red, was: *La amistad de nuestros paises se fortalece diariamente* (The Friendship of Our Countries Strengthens Every Day). Under this was a photo, with Ho Chi Minh's bust in the background, of Raúl Castro shaking hands with Vietnam's Secretary General Nguyen Phu Trong. The story covered Raúl's Vietnam visit to reaffirm ties with that nation.

Leafing through the paper I read the national headlines:

Energy Saving Improvements in Fishing Industry	Ramiro Valdés Evaluates Important Economic and Social Works
Machado Confirms State of July 26 Preparations	Emergency Repairs for Canal Magistral ZaZa
Dietary Fiber Suggestions	Technical Education in Tune with Needs of Capital

Then the international headlines:

Al Assad Accuses U.S. of
Helping Armed Groups
Evo Morales Emphasizes
New Bolivian Armed
Forces Image
Putin Declares National
Mourning Following
Southern Russia Disaster
Protests in Pakistan against
Reopening of NATO Routes

California Protests against Safe
Community Anti-Immigrant
Plan
Venezuela Celebrates
Ophthalmology Program
Anniversary
Italian Gross Domestic Product
to Fall

There was the sports page and finally the back page, which had the following:

Development Project Realized

Advances in National Truck Load
Deliveries

The front page of perhaps the world's most boring newspaper, *Granma,* **named after "the yacht that brought Fidel and his little friends to Cuba from Mexico."**

In a poor country of 11.5 million people, there was not a single murder, traffic accident, rape, kidnapping, robbery, mugging or burglary. There was only news of constant advances and improvements. Nothing domestic was ever wrong and if it was close to being wrong it was being remedied or improved. The only bad news happened in foreign countries and all bad news were the result of actions by countries that were enemies of Cuba.

I wondered at the level of intelligence that the writers of this paper assumed in their readers. If they expected to be believed, it couldn't have been very high, or else they counted on indoctrination to pull it off. If the bar clientele's reaction to my quip, "Now I can really get to the truth about the world," as I exited the bar could be taken as a survey, this rag was fooling no one. The *Granma* mirrors the grand farce that is Cuba. It is a vulgar simpleton's attempt at sustaining an obvious fiction, a sort of embarrassing faux pas few dare laugh at. It might have been the paper resting on the center table of Winston Smith's apartment in George Orwell's *1984*, the great novel inspired while Orwell witnessed the repression and purges perpetrated by the Republican side under the influence of competing communist and anarchist groups in 1937 Barcelona. Contrary to what my university students assured me in 1985 Spain, the United States was not Orwell's Big Brother. Instead, it was Josef Stalin and his ilk. Orwell clarified his stance on totalitarianism when he wrote in *The Observer* in 1944: "The essential fact about a totalitarian regime is that it has no laws. People are not punished for specific offenses, but because they are considered to be politically or intellectually undesirable. What they have done or not done is irrelevant."

At this thought, I decided to go to a big bookstore I had passed by before in order to check if they had *1984*. At the bookstore I went to the classic novel section; of course, it wasn't in the shelves. Then I went to a counter pretending I wanted to order it, but the agent had not even heard of it (a bookstore agent who has never heard of one of the greatest, best-known novels of the 20th century?), nor was it on the list of books one could order. I knew it was going to be exactly as it turned out, but I had to confirm it. No doubt Orwell's vision of the dark world ruled by totalitarian governments that behaved much like the Cuban regime, *Big Brother, doublethink, thoughtcrime*, and all, was too close for comfort. The *1984* reader would have pegged the Committees for the Defense of the Revolution as the Thought Police and the *Granma* would be all too recognizable as the organ of the Ministry of Truth. Instead, I bought a book of Cuban poetry and left.

I purposely skipped lunch looking forward to the good dinner I expected that evening at the restaurant Eli had recommended. I spent the rest of the daylight hours walking around Old Havana, having several Cuban coffees, an espresso-strength sugared potion in a miniature cup, at sidewalk cafés and reading the poetry of my countrymen. Occasionally, I'd rest my eyes on the alluring walk of Cuban women who sauntered by. The walk is, in fact, famous throughout Latin America. It is a sashay that combines sensuousness, indifference, grace, sassiness and, somehow, demureness all in one, yet it is not too much and not too little; it's just right. Inspired by the poets I was reading and the provocative grace of their walk, I decided to write a poem in its honor:

Mujer

Te deslizas
Por una cuerda floja de flores
Como si el poder y el impulso de tu cuerpo
Ardieran en tus caderas
Que en acecho de gata agarran el espacio
Y lo arrojan en seda hacia el pasado
Dejando en el aire estelas de sueños
Que bailan con un fantasma que vive del ojo del hombre
Un algo ligero de polvo y rocío
Pero tan sólido que mueve mundos

Woman

You glide by
On a tightrope of lilies
As if the power and impulse of your body
Blazed within your hips
Which in your cat's stalk snatch up space
And sling it back to the past in filaments of silk
Leaving the air with a wake of dreams
That dance with a ghost that lives off the eyes of men
Something light made of dust and dew
Yet so solid that it moves the world

That evening I met Eli at 8:00 at the front door of the guesthouse. He was happy to see me, as if he'd doubted I'd remember. Ten minutes later we were at El Guajirito, the restaurant with the Flamenco show. He led me upstairs to a rustic but chic interior salon with tables before a stage.

"This is the restaurant," he said, "I'll wait for you at the bar over here."

"Why don't you join me at the table?"

"Thank you, but this is a privately owned place and I'm not dressed well enough to sit at the restaurant. But at the bar it's OK."

"Well let's go to the bar and I'll buy you a drink while you wait." At the bar, I ordered a beer for both from a lovely bartender, like all the waitresses, dressed in an almost tutu-like mini skirt and a cowboy hat. "So this is privately owned?" I asked Eli.

"Yes, it's one of the changes that Raúl has allowed and you'll taste the difference in the food."

"Well, let's order something then." I called for a menu and ordered a plate and another beer for Eli while he waited at the bar. Then I went into the restaurant and another beauty led me to a table in front of the stage.

I ordered a Cuban classic, *ropa vieja* (literally, old clothes), a pulled beef dish with fried plantains and rice. Minutes later a serpentine oboe filled the air and I knew I wasn't in for flamenco. Sure enough, it was belly dancing and soon I was chewing a decent *ropa vieja* to the rhythm of the ample swaying hips of a troupe of Cuban ladies in Arab belly dance garb. "Capitalism," I muttered to myself, not without a hint of disdain.

Before my trip, an American friend who had recently visited the island had told me that Cubans were not allowed to speak at length to foreigners. This was confirmed by the conversation I'd had with the old man in the park. However, there was a part of me that was still shocked when I experienced this again that evening, worth describing in detail because what happened also displayed the charm, inventiveness and recourse of the Cuban people.

Eli was pedaling me back to the guesthouse after dinner. We went by a corner bar whose music spilled onto the street from a flute led band. Many people were milling outside around the bar's windows, listening to the music and looking in. I told Eli to pull over so we could

63

have a drink and a listen. I let Eli take the lead into the place. At the door, a big bouncer gave me the once over then slowly closed and opened his eyelids in consent. Eli went straight to a table in the middle where two young women sat. He asked permission to sit and they nodded with that certain chin-up dignity of whores. We sat down and introduced ourselves. The girl in her late twenties to my right was Gretel; the younger one across from me with her back to the band was Yorleny. Eli sat to my left; I asked him to order four mojitos.

The actual bar sprawled along the wall that faced the corner entrance and the street side. Above the woodwork brimming with liquor, an ancient brass sign read "Bar Monserrate." The band at the back wall sprouted the sassy procession of flowers that is Cuban music and hanging above it a large flat-screen TV showed an international friendly between the Cuban national baseball team and an American squad visiting the island. "Who are you for?" I asked the ladies nodding at the screen. "Cuba! Of course!" cried Yorleny and right after she said it, she jiggled her buxom breasts to the sudden entrance of the maracas. Eli and I had to burst out laughing and from then on the party was on as the waiter arrived with the mojitos. We clinked glasses and took such a drag on the cocktails that when we set them down they were half empty. I shouted at the waiter, "*Camarero!* Four more!" while raising my glass and holding up four fingers. Then I looked at Yorleny again and noticed her eyes were an incongruent blue for the mixed-race beauty she was.

"Those can't be real," I said pursing my lips at her eyes.

She frowned, looked down at her boobs and said, "Of course they are!" Then magically the maracas returned and without missing a beat she shook hers, so to speak, and cried, "See!" We all nearly fell out of our chairs at that one.

The new round of mojitos came just as we were finishing the first. "Here's to the mojitos!" I toasted, raising my glass.

"No, here's to what the mojitos do to us!" chimed in Gretel. We clinked glasses as she said, "Chin-chin," the onomatopoeia for the sound.

After we all took a good pull on the drinks I said, "We just drank to small penises!"

"Never! I would never drink to those!" cried Gretel. "Really?"

"I'm afraid we did. Chin-chin means a little boy's penis in Japanese."

"Here's to little penises! Chin-chin!" toasted Yorleny as we chin-chinned again.

I looked at Eli, his face in a no-man's-land between agony and ecstasy. "He's not used to this," I thought. But me? After the nightlife in Japan with its hostess clubs, I was content to enjoy the company of women, buying them drinks and keeping it light, but nothing else. I was like an old Chihuahua with a dinosaur bone, maybe not totally up to the task, but I knew how to gnaw. "You OK?" I asked him.

"OK. But you know these are whores…"

I looked wide-eyed at Gretel and at Yorleny, then back at him and said, "Noooo, no way!" Eli smiled, jabbed me with his elbow and raised his glass.

"You're the Devil!"

"Thanks! But you know the old saying, the Devil is more a devil because he's old than because he's the Devil!" The band struck a salsa and Yorleny yelled out, "Didi!" A young mulatto strode over to the table,

"At the door a big bouncer gave me the once over then slowly closed and opened his eyelids in consent." The bouncer is at the far left watching the door. The de rigueur attire of Cuban waiters seems to be a white shirt, vest, and a bow tie.

nodded at me for permission, took Yorleny's hand and led her to the space between the tables. He spun her, her smile flashing like a lighthouse gone mad. Didi led her in the weave of movements of the dance, the crowd's eyes all on them now, and Yorleny let herself be maneuvered like a Ferrari on a mountain road. The band ended the piece in a long rustle of the maracas, Didi bending her backward in a sweep, her hair grazing the floor. The crowd exploded in applause. Didi led the winded Yorleny back to the table, bowed to me and swaggered off to the bar.

"What a dancer Didi is! And you too, Yorleny! *Felicidades*!" We all raised our glasses and drank.

"That's what Didi does for a living. He dances for tips and drinks at nightclubs," said Gretel. Pointing at my glass and then at Didi at the bar, I signaled to the waiter to get Didi a mojito.

In the meantime, Eli had been talking to Yorleny. Then he turned to me and said, "The ladies want to know which one you'd prefer for a roll in the hay."

"Well, I don't know. You know I *am* a good boy, after all," I teased.

"So what? I'm a good girl too," said Gretel.

"Not me," said Yorleny, "I like the Devil!" This time she didn't wait for the maracas and shook her boobs with special vigor. Just then a tall black man came to the table between Gretel and me and showed us a deck of cards, tapped it and with the same hand drew a question mark in the air. I nodded. Communicating only with his elegant hands he put on the greatest display of magic I had ever seen up close and in person. Working cards, puffballs, and handkerchiefs, he mesmerized us for five minutes without uttering a word in a whirl of sleight of hand. Of course, I tipped him well. He bowed with a smile and went off to the table behind us where two Brits now sat. "Is he deaf and dumb?" I asked Gretel.

"No, it's the show; he only speaks through his hands for the show."

Then the bar and the multitude outside roared as the Cuban national team scored the winning run in the bottom of the ninth to beat the Americans. I ordered more mojitos and we drank to the victory. After a tête-à-tête with Yorleny, Eli turned to me and said the girls still wanted to know if you were interested in you know what. To make it simple and so as not to put off the ladies, I lied, telling him that in all the excitement I had spent most of the cash I was carrying. So explaining my cash shortage, I told the ladies we'd try to come again tomorrow. They nodded in agreement and I ordered another round.

The drinks came and while Yorleny was already approaching the two Brits and Eli was away in the toilet, I started a conversation with Gretel. After getting a good sample of her discourse, I said, "Your accent and word choice isn't from the street. You seem well educated."

"That's because I am. I'm an engineer."

"Don't tell me, you got sick of the lousy salary and so you turned to this."

She leveled her large brown eyes at me and said, "That about says it all. I have a son and I need more money not only for him but also to help my parents."

"How do you feel about having to do this?"

"I'm still young and pretty enough that I can pick my clients and then it's not so bad as some women have it. They have to pick whoever comes along. I'd really hate it if I were forced to do that. Some men are disgusting or you can tell they're mean."

"Am I one of those?" I asked, fishing.

"I would have left this table long ago if I thought you were."

"I was just fishing. I know what I am." I looked around and said, "I left this place long before you were born and even being a boy I remember how it was. Let me tell you, this, all this, could be much, much better. This country, these people, my people, you, you deserve much better than this." She nodded in agreement, but as she did so, she was looking warily askance at something behind me.

"Listen, I have to go," she said, her eyes meeting mine again.

"Why so suddenly?"

"There's a cop at the door and he's had his eye on me for a while now."

"So what? You haven't done anything."

"Talking to you is enough."

"So what would happen if you didn't leave?"

"He'd take me away and interrogate me... Unless I did something for him." She said this with her hand leaning on her cheek as if to hide her mouth. "Look, I'm going to get up as if I were going to the toilet, so don't stand up to kiss me goodbye. Act like I'm coming right back.

Or better yet, just look away and start talking to Eli for a moment and when you turn back I'll be gone."

"I understand," I turned to Eli, and the corner of my eye felt her leave. I explained everything that had just happened then asked him, "What would he have done to her? She was quite worried."

"There's a back door here past the bathroom, lucky for her. The cop would have taken her to the station and interrogated her about the conversation; you were talking to her—how do you say it—not casually. A lot of these guys read lips, you know. Or he might have made her suck him or whatever to let her go."

"Poor girl. Someone told me about this. So it's still that bad."

"That's the way it's always been. But you know that."

"Yes, but I've been away where nothing like this happens and I guess it still took me by surprise. Now I'm wondering if the cop was actually following me and maybe he wanted to find out what we were talking about from her to get to me. What do you think?"

"Maybe, I wouldn't bet against it. They've probably been watching or following you all along. Either way it's the same result, they would have taken her away to find out what you were talking about."

"I can't believe these bastards. Let's go, Eli, it's been a great time, but now I'm a little tired, not to mention broke."

Eli turned to say goodbye to Yorleny, who had been distracted by the Brits. Then he went out the door. I hesitated a moment, soaking in her beauty, that effortless charm of Cuban women. Yorleny stood up, came and sat down in the chair next to me. She slowly leaned forward and put her face up close, leveled her eyes on mine and said, "You are not young, but not old. Do you do it with gusto still?"

"With you, with gusto, still."

"Please come tomorrow with more cash and less thirst, OK?"

Of course, I never saw her again.

Day Five

I woke up with a mild hangover as the morning sun and the din of life from the street below poured into the room. Eli had dropped me off in the wee hours and I remembered through a cobweb that I had agreed to meet him at 10:30 that morning; he was going to show me the sights of Old Havana.

Sure enough, he was waiting at the door smiling his tired smile. "I want you to meet some relatives of mine before we go; they live right around the corner." I got in his bicitaxi and we went all of fifty meters to a house around the corner. Answering Eli's calling, a middle-aged couple, Luis and Glenda, greeted us at the door. "This is the friend I was telling you about," said Eli. Glenda was in her fifties, a plump white woman with thick glasses that bloated her eyes. Luis, a tall, corpulent man of around sixty also of Spanish ancestry extended his hand and said, "Welcome," as I shook it.

I was invited to sit at a table in a dark and cluttered room with ancient furniture. An old pedal-run Singer sewing machine sat in the corner. While Luis busied himself making coffee, Eli was explaining to them about me. When they understood the nature of my background they turned into a sort of conversational tag-team.

"So you haven't been back in 50 years? Well, let me tell you, not much has changed," said Luis. "We're no better off than we were then and just like then we're still poor and just barely make it every month."

"That's life here for most people," cut in Glenda, "Just enough to scrape by every month. Luis is a retired stevedore and I'm a seamstress (chin-pointing at the Singer). I still work mostly fixing used clothes; nobody has money to buy new cloth. But if we didn't have that, I don't know how we'd get by."

"My pension is 240 pesos a month," mourned Luis.

"What's that, $10 a month? What in the world can you buy for that?"

Luis stood up and went to a shelf, returning with a dog-eared little booklet. "Look, this is the *Libreta de Abastecimiento* you've heard about. It's been getting smaller and smaller every year. These days you get four pounds of sugar, seven pounds of rice, five eggs, 10 ounces of beans, 10 of oil, four ounces of coffee, half a pound of chicken—or fish when available, and a kilo of salt per family of four. This lasts about a week."

"And how much does that cost?"

"About a dollar per person," said Glenda. "And now Raúl is talking about getting rid of it!"

"So that's one tenth of your pension that goes for food and it lasts a week? How do you make it to the end of the month?" I asked.

"Let me tell you how we get by each month, Glenda does a job here and there, we borrow from relatives and neighbors, I do odd jobs, we improvise to stretch the food, we buy stolen food cheap, some people cultivate gardens and raise chickens, we barter things..."

"And if you knew what we went through when the Russians pulled the plug!" said Glenda, "People were eating grass and bark in this country, some ate leather."

"Some even would take an old rag, wash it, rinse it, pour flour on it and just to fill the hole in their stomachs fry it up as a meal!" said Luis.

"Then in the middle of the night people started going after the government cows and pigs and butchering them," said Glenda.

"So then the most ridiculous thing happened. This is the only country in the world where the penalty for killing a cow is more severe than for killing a human being. The minimum sentence for murdering a cow is 13 years, for a human being it's eight!"

"It's an upside down world you're describing. It maddens me to think about it."

"It maddens you and it consumes us," said Luis. "But if you watch these sons of whores in action you realize that they are the ones that eat well and dress well. But you can't complain."

Glenda cut in, "There's a joke about a tourist who came here and asked a Cuban couple what they thought about the Revolution and what it has accomplished.

'We can't complain,' said one of the Cubans.

'Then everything is OK, right?' asked the tourist.

'No, it's just that we *really can't* complain.'"

I chuckled, but I immediately sobered when I realized looking at Luis' face that it was a bitter joke.

"These bastards will disappear you if you talk against them. You've heard of the CDR, haven't you?"

"Sure, the Committees for the Defense of the Revolution."

"Well then, you know that all it is is a nationwide neighborhood spy network. A bunch of stool pigeons that live among us, reporting any "irregularities" to the bastards in power. How many *cubanitos* (literally, little Cubans) have fallen to these ass-licking scumbags! I tell you this is why this has become a nation of ventriloquists. Those guys are even taught to lip read so that you find yourself talking out of the corner of your mouth if you're mentioning an irregularity in public."

"I know all that you're telling me and you're right, nothing has changed since I left, except now I see prostitutes everywhere. Wasn't this what Fidel railed against: that the Americans had turned Cuba into a brothel?"

"It's still illegal," said Glenda, "but they can't stop it and I think many in the government realize that it's the only way some women can make a decent wage. So they wink at it."

"The long and the short of it is that this country is a great farce," said Luis, "and you wouldn't believe how many people feel they've wasted their lives here."

"Look maybe my coming here has depressed you. I'm sorry."

"Not at all, it actually feels good to be able to tell someone from the outside," said Glenda.

"This is indeed a strange confessional; instead of your sins, you're confessing someone else's." They chuckled at my observation. "But look, I promise you that what you've told me here today will go towards more than just venting your frustrations. I'm going to write about this and try to publish it. Your story, the real story about Cuba has to be told. Lenin once said, "We can always count on our useful idiots in the West" (to work our propaganda) and you wouldn't believe how much of the regime's propaganda I hear back in Costa Rica."

"Like what?" asked Luis.

"Like that the best doctors in the world are Cuban."

"What a joke!" said Luis.

"What madness!" cried Glenda.

"You go to any neighborhood clinic here," Luis continued, "and it's dirty and has hardly any equipment. You wait and wait and when the doctor finally sees you, he tries to get rid of you as quickly as possible. He does a perfunctory examination then his eternal solution is to give you some pills. It's free, but pretty worthless health care. The doctors, like the rest of the government employees, are not accountable and if you're misdiagnosed, that's just too bad. Better luck next time."

"That's what I figured. People also rave about the free education even up to the university level."

"Free? Sure it's free—while you're studying. But then, university graduates have to spend three years working free for the government, who decides where they will send them to work. That's three years after graduation working for free! So, is it free?"

"Of course not," I said, "People forget the real purpose of education is to open your mind, increase your opportunities in life and teach you how to think well enough to be in charge of your life and influence society. But what good is education if it's used so that you can read only what they want you to read? Or if education has little impact on getting ahead in life. My cleaning lady is a licensed schoolteacher and I was just talking to an engineer yesterday who has turned to prostitution. Then the other day I learned that the taxi drivers are the new rich!"

"Why waste your time," said Glenda, "spending years studying if all you're going to get is $10 a month more at the end of your three years of free work for the government?"

"Not only that," continued Luis, "you wouldn't believe what hoops the government makes you jump through in order to qualify for higher education. First as a kid they want you to belong to the Unión de Pioneros de Cuba (Union of Pioneers of Cuba) and you're forced to march in front of the U.S. Interests Section or do all kinds of things to promote the Revolution for free. You have to do a tour of duty with the army. Then your parents have to belong to the Communist Party, the CDR, the CTC (the Confederation of Cuban Workers). You have to have a spotless record doing free revolutionary work for the government and all of these activities are kept in a dossier called the Cumulative Student File. So much for free education."

"But you have to admit," I said, "political motives aside, that if there is anything that the Revolution has accomplished, it is the universal education of the Cuban people."

"That is without question," replied Luis, "but was it necessary to turn this place into a totalitarian state in order to do that?"

Soon after this exchange, we bid a heartfelt goodbye and left.

Out in the late morning sunshine, Eli pedaled me to La Bodeguita del Medio, a little hole-in-the-wall bar that specialized in one of Hemingway's two favorite Cuban drinks, the mojito and the daiquirí. A crowd of tourists milled about outside taking photos. Past the entrance and a four-man band playing *¿Y tu qué has hecho?* (And What Have You Done?), an old tune included in the Buena Vista Social Club album. I jostled my way to the counter and ordered a mojito. On the wall over the bar shelf full of Havana Club rum was a framed blotched poster with Hemingway's large cursive handwriting. It said:

My mojito in La Bodeguita

My daiquirí in El Floridita

Ernest Hemingway

I took a hard pull on the mojito and in an instant its fire rocked me. The sun angled through the front window lighting on the backs of the musicians who sang:

En el tronco de un arbol una niña	On the trunk of a tree a little girl
Grabó su nombre henchida de placer	Filled with pleasure carved her name
Y el arbol conmovido allá en su seno	And the tree its heart so deeply moved
A la niña una flor dejó caer	Let drop a flower for the little girl
Yo soy el arbol conmovido y triste	I am that tree so moved and sad
Tú eres la niña que mi tronco hirió	You are the little girl that hurt my trunk
Yo guardo siempre tu querido nombre	Your dear name I have always kept
¿Y tú que has hecho de mi pobre flor?	And you, what have you done with my poor flower?

In his moments of happiness, my father used to sing this charming old song of unrequited love. I felt a swelling in my eyes, then a tickle on my cheeks, and I realized I was crying, crying for my dear dead father, my lost country, and everything that might have been, but never was. Images from 1961 flooded back...

One morning in April of 1961, a thunder in the distance rattled and fluttered the French windows and awakened us. Thinking it was a morning storm, I looked out the window but sunlight bathed the veranda. The thunder struck again and this time shook the windows and the earth. "Those are bombs," said father as he got up and turned on the radio. Immediately an agitated voice flooded the room, "... aradas, an aerial attack has been reported at Ciudad Libertad in Havana... "Consuelo, my God, here come the Americans!" But it was not to be. The bombing of the airfield at the old military barracks was one of many diversions

The musicians at La Bodeguita del Medio playing ¿Y tu qué has hecho? as I walked in the door. No microphones, just three men playing as honestly as three men can play.

from the landing of 1,500 exiled counter-revolutionaries at a desolate beach 100 kilometers southeast of Havana called the Bay of Pigs. Abandoned by air support, they were pinned at that beach until surrender. Far from overthrowing Castro, the defeated exiles strengthened him. Kennedy traded tractors and medicine for a thousand prisoners as an iron grip descended on the island. And on some days when the wind was cruel, it carried from across the harbor the faint crack of the fusillades.

One night after over a year's wait, a courier came to the guest house and interrupted father's conversations with Mr. Faycund. "Don Facundo," said the courier, "I was sent to deliver your visa." My father, straining to contain his joy, took the document and thanked the man. To inconvenience and stifle preparation, they had scheduled us to leave Cuba the next day. "Consuelo, boys, we have to get ready. Tomorrow we fly to America and freedom!"

The flight was at noon; the tickets had been prepaid along with the visa application. Because only one suitcase per person was allowed on the flight, the six suitcases we'd brought to Havana had to be reduced to four. We also had learned that anything of value was confiscated at the airport. And so that night turned into a ruthless elimination. We discarded all stuff of emotional value in favor of that of need. Photographs, jewelry, ancient books, heirlooms, fine clothing and shoes, a camera, an oil paint set, paintings, notebooks, diaries all felt the ax. Near dawn, the four suitcases stood on the floor, portable monuments to the indispensable. We went to sleep for a few hours and woke up in time for breakfast. The jewelry and most of what was of value was left with a trusted neighbor who promised to send everything through the Mexican embassy. The rest we destroyed if too personal and if not, it was given away to house guests.

"You look like a boxer. Were you ever a boxer?"

I turned to my right to see the beaten black mug of an ex-boxer about my age looking me over. He was drinking a mojito. "No, I never boxed. Why do you say I look like a boxer?"

"Broad shoulders, long arms, leaned forward a bit. Like a boxer."

"You forgot to mention my crooked nose. But no, sorry, never boxed, played Capoeira, though, when younger."

"What's that?"

"A Brazilian martial art."

"I was a boxer."

"You look like a boxer."

"Boxed my whole life for Cuba."

"You heard Teofilio Stevenson died recently?"

"Ah, you know Teofilio!"

"Of course, I know Teofilio, one of the greatest heavyweights ever."

"What do you mean one of? He was the greatest heavyweight ever."

"Not with a guy named Muhammad Ali on the same planet."

"He was a pussy. Spent his life running away." He said this with a glint of mirth in his eyes.

"I can't believe my ears! You're actually standing here next to me telling me Muhammad Ali was a pussy? Let me see," I patted my cheeks then the counter. "No, I'm still here." Then I looked at the mojito. "Maybe it's the mojito, I drank one too many mojitos."

"Not only was he a pussy he boxed like a pussy. What the hell do you call this?" He put up his dukes imitating Ali's boxing stance, right fist up by his chin, left arm down by his waist. That's how a pussy boxes, like he's afraid you're going to hit him in the balls."

"No, you have it all wrong. *This* is how a pussy fights." I put up my dukes assuming the classic boxer's stance of Teofilio Stevenson—both fists up, the left more extended, the left shoulder raised a bit to cover the chin's left side, head down, eyes up. "This is a pussy that's so slow he's worried about getting hit on the chin! Ali was so fast, he didn't need to cover up with his left!" By this time, everyone around us was listening as the band played on.

"You lied to me," he said in a deadpan, "I thought you said you didn't box."

"I just said I never boxed. I didn't say I didn't know anything about boxing."

"Angel, get this guy a mojito on me."

"Sure, why not, thank you."

While Angel was making us the mojitos, the former boxer said, "We had a good one going didn't we? Of course, I was kidding you about Ali."

"Really? I wasn't kidding you about Teofilio! He really was a pussy!" He burst out laughing, patting me on the back. We drank up the mojitos and I counter-invited him to another round. He had been a middleweight all his life, was even an alternate for the Olympics, but never did go although he'd been a well-known boxer in his day. We finally introduced ourselves when I told him I had to leave as Eli was still waiting outside. His name was Jorge. Before I left I asked him, "Jorge, OK, really now, who do you think was the greatest ever?"

"Without question, Muhammad Ali." We laughed together and

high-fived in parting. Cuba is full of characters like this. The Cuban people are well known in Latin America for being *simpáticos*.

I got myself together, bought a Montecristo No. 5 on the way out and met Eli on the street. Taking 20 CUCs out and putting them in his hand, I said, "Eli, I know I can trust you to give Glenda and Luis this present. They need it dearly and I didn't want to give it to them in person because I could tell they would have refused because of pride and all that." He looked at me sadly, took the money and thanked me on their behalf. "Aren't you hungry, Eli? I'm starving."

"I know just the place," said my faithful *bicitaxista*, "It's La Cervecería in La Plaza Vieja (Old Square). Good food, good beer."

"What could be wrong?" said I.

Ten minutes after pedaling through Calle Obispo, the main tourist street in Old Havana, a large plaza the size of a football field blossomed from the narrow street. A fountain stood in the middle, surrounded on all sides by pastel buildings several stories high. Arcades skirted the perimeter of the plaza. On the corner as we entered was La Cervecería. A band with a woman flute lead played by the entrance and the place teemed with tourists from the world over. The scent of grilled pork and seafood wafted by us as a waiter carried a tray full to one of the many tables sprouting umbrellas near the entrance. I heard Eli's stomach rumble in its depths. "This time you're sitting with me," I said. "Let's sit down at that table."

We sat down at one of the umbrella-shaded tables that jutted into the square. A waiter in a bow tie and vest attended us immediately. He recommended the special of the day, skewer-grilled pork and seafood. I ordered a light beer for Eli and an amber one for myself. The beers came and we toasted and drank deeply. Refreshed and re-energized, I started looking around to see what to photograph from the table. A couple in the famous white garb of the santeristas, the Cuban version of the Haitian voodoo practitioners, approached, crossing the square. I focused on the woman to shoot, but she frowned and put her hand up to cover her face as I pressed the shutter.

"Some Santeristas don't like to be photographed; they think you steal a part of their soul," said Eli.

The big plates arrived sizzling. Eli's mouth dropped open as his eyes fell on the four grilled lobster, prawn, pork loin and scallop skewers served on a bed of steaming rice and salad on the side. It looked like such a departure from what I had so far tried in Havana restaurants that I asked Eli, "This wouldn't be one of those new privately owned businesses that Raúl has allowed recently, would it?"

My question caught Eli with his fork already on its way into his mouth. He hesitated a moment, then plunged the lobster into the aperture anyway: he had decided to answer me with his mouth full. "Yes," he replied thinly and chewed away, his eyes half closed and out of focus. Just then I realized that Eli had lost contact with the external world.

"Of course," I continued, "that's how come this food is so wonderful: the owner really cares what people say about his restaurant."

"Yes."

I finally tasted a scallop and Eli had by then disappeared an entire skewer.

Then I tried an experiment. "This is really terrible food isn't it, Eli?"

"Yes."

Then I understood I had lost him completely. So I turned away busying myself with the food, the music, and girl-watching as Eli made sounds akin to those made in the throes of sex by people not preoccupied with chewing. "Poor man," I thought, "he's not had decent food in a long time."

"That's the best food I've had in a long time!" Exclaimed Eli, putting down his fork and knife as I was half way done with my plate.

"Welcome back, Eli."

"What do you mean?"

"Never mind. What's next on the agenda?"

We finished lunch. I bought the band's CD from the flutist who came around the tables during a break. We then walked across the square to a corner building that formed one of the four points of the Plaza Vieja. We took the elevator to the eighth floor where there was a camera obscura observatory of Old Havana at the top. Along with at least a dozen tourists, we crammed into a dark room at the center of which lay a six-foot diameter bowl mirror that reflected the image cast by another bowl mirror above it on the roof. The bowl around which everyone milled reversed the inverted image cast by the roof mirror, rendering a 360° real-time view of Havana Harbor and Havana Vieja. The announced language for the "tour" was French. A middle-aged toad-like mulatta with a long baton entered the room and climbed atop a wooden pedestal before the bowl. She embarked upon her explanation of the reflected scene in a flat imperious tone with the most horrendous Spanish-accented French I had ever heard in all my years; the French throat-pronounced "r" she turned into the Spanish double "rr" and the French diphthonged vowels she simplified to the nearest sounding Spanish open vowel.

"*Vuala le Chato du Morrrrro*," she boomed, "*et ici nus avon le Malecon, la grande promenade le long de la merrr des Carrraibes. Le Chato du Morrro et la ancienne forrrterrresse du...*" It was quite comical. But no matter how much she pointed at only the major landmarks, one couldn't avoid seeing what was in between: the wreck of Old Havana, the roofless, dilapidated buildings, the drab gray of neglect, the ravages of erosion. It occurred to me that our guide (like the rest of her generation and, now after all these years, the government) had become so inured to the wreck that they didn't see that foreigners might think it were less than dignified.

"*Et vuala La Havane Vielle d'odjurd'hui!*" The woman ended with a flourish.

"*Très bien fait, mademoiselle!*" I heard myself say in a tone that only I knew was sarcastic and everyone started to applaud the horrible performance.

"*Merrci bocu*," replied the guide, convinced of her prowess.

Out in the brilliant sunshine again, Eli took me to Havana Harbor, the inlet whose entrance is a narrow strait between where the Malecón begins and Morro Castle. By the harbor was a huge building that was once a warehouse for unloading merchant ships. It had been turned into an art market for Cuban artists who sold their paintings, sculptures, jewelry and trinkets. Of course, only tourists bought anything as almost everything on sale was at least a month's wage. I bought an abstract ebony statuette of a woman and two bracelets for my girlfriend and her mother back in Costa Rica. The bracelets were silver plated forks, probably abandoned by some rich family that had long ago fled the island, that had been bent into an oval and whose teeth had been twisted to mount semiprecious stones. The result was a slip-on bracelet with a Dalíesque motif that was another testament to the creativity of Cubans.

Later we went to visit the house on Paula Street where José Martí was born in 1853. This was Cuba's great liberator-poet, writer of the lyrics to Cuba's national song, *Guantanamera*. It was a simple two-story middle-class home painted beige and iridescent blue. The regime has adopted the great man's name in its quest for legitimacy, claiming that what it had turned Cuba into was precisely what Martí had intended. Nothing could be further from the truth. Although Martí lived for a while in the United States and did express his misgivings about the imperialistic intents it had towards Cuba, he was an admirer of, as he said himself, "the immigrant-based society, whose principal aspiration is to construct a truly modern country, based upon hard work and progressive ideas."[1] Martí marveled at the meritocracy and utter freedom of speech that is the foundation of American culture. A pragmatic classical liberal, Martí would turn in his grave if he knew

The house where José Martí, Cuba's liberator from Spain, was born. The regime has claimed his posthumous support although in reality he was an admirer of the U.S. and its culture.

how the Castro brothers had twisted his words to fit communist ideology. Later, I visited a bookstore in Old Havana to find out what writings of his were on sale; I found none that dealt with the United States or that were published while he was there.

Eli asked me if I cared to visit some friends of his nearby. We pedaled a few blocks to a four-story building. As we climbed the stairs to the roof where his friends lived he confided that I could speak freely with his friends—"They don't like the government." At the top, he led me through a squalid little apartment that opened onto the roof, which functioned as the living room, furnished with plastic garden chairs. It was a couple, Ernesto and Consuelo, and Consuelo's cousin Enrique. All were in their 30's and of the swarthy complexion that is the result of generations of mixture between black and white. I could see suspicion in their eyes at my appearance, as if they doubted I was really Cuban. After exchanging the usual niceties and under the influence of a few rums with lime soda, Enrique said, "You know the last thing I would have guessed is that you were originally from here."

"People in Costa Rica tell me the same thing. I guess it's that my parents were children of Galicians, who are not of Mediterranean ancestry, but Celts, the fair-haired and clear-eyed people from what is today Scotland, Ireland, and Wales. Did you know that the national instrument of Galicia is the bagpipe? An ancient simpler version of the modern Scottish one. The word *castro*, the name of our fearless leaders, also of Galician ancestry, refers to the 5,000-year-old circular stone base and thatched roof dwellings the Celts built along the coast of Galicia. If you go to Galicia today you'd see why the Celts colonized it. The land looks green like Scotland or Ireland and it's just as rainy, except that it's warmer."

"Well that explains your looks," said Enrique. "Now I know why here we call white Cubans *gallegos* (Galicians)."

"Living in Costa Rica I know that the stereotype of the average Cuban is a black or mulatto. And you know what, now that I'm here fifty years later I remember Cuba used to be a whiter country."

"I've thought about that," said Eli, "Most of the people that left in the 60's were the white oligarchy. Your family was part of that group?"

"If by oligarchy you mean a small ruling elite, then it wasn't. My father was a lawyer and landowner, yes, but he wasn't involved in the government. But if you mean the wealthy minority, then I have to admit

The original *castros* in Santa Terra, Galicia, in northwest Spain. The stone dwellings were built about 5,000 years ago by Celts who colonized a land that was green like Scotland or Ireland and just as rainy, except that it was warmer.

that my family was quite privileged and we were part of the "oligarchy" if you will."

"How much land did your family have?" asked Ernesto.

"My father's father came to Cuba penniless from Galicia toward the end of the 19th century. But he worked hard and soon saved enough to start a business with some associates. He married into a wealthy family and soon bought 2,800 acres near Holguín. He turned that land into a farm, which my father, along with his brother and sister, inherited. My father being the oldest and most capable took charge of it and developed it further."

"So what happened to the farm?" asked Consuelo.

"As you can imagine, the government confiscated it in '61. The old man received a letter one day that told him his land now belonged to the government, and that was that. And this was after he, like everyone at that time, had supported Castro, never suspecting that he would turn communist."

"What did you produce in that farm?" asked Consuelo.

"Just about everything, but mostly cane and cattle. I understand that the Castros have really cut back on sugar production; is that true?"

"Yes, it's true," answered Ernesto.

"Finally," I said. "You know this was always the problem with the Cuban economy. What did the Spaniards do to their colonies? After the gold and silver were mined out, they turned their colonies into

82

Family portrait of my father's side of the family, circa 1927. From rear left to right: Grandfather Facundo, Grandmother Consuelo, Uncle Jillo, Aunt Nena, and my father, Facundo Jr. Grandfather came to Cuba penniless and built a small fortune. Jillo would spend eight years in Castro's prisons on suspicion of being a counter-revolutionary.

Cuban cowboys, circa 1958. My brother, Facundo Jr., or Facundito (left), and I at the old *finca* before it was confiscated in 1961. Our mother would end up stuffing the title to the farm in between the seat cushions of the then Rancho Boyeros International Airport so that they would not cancel our tickets to freedom.

huge farms for European commodities that did not feed the people: sugar, tobacco, coffee, rubber. Cuba became a huge sugar cane farm— hardly a healthy diversified economy. So what did the great economist, Fidel Castro, do for over 40 years? He made Cuba even more dependent on sugar. Maybe you guys are too young, but Eli must remember what Fidel did at the end of the 60's."

"I remember. He made us work like dogs to reach his big ten million ton harvest by the end of the decade. Never made it, but we were working for nothing like slaves out in the hot sun."

"And you know why, Eli? The oldest reason in the world: money. The Russians for years paid Castro five times the world price of sugar. So it was logical. But that's not what an anti-colonial, anti-imperialist government is supposed to do. With complete control of the country, this "great man" did nothing to make Cuba self-sufficient and turned it into an even bigger puppet economy, this time for the Russians. Anyone tell you about these little details?"

"What? That the Russians were paying that much for our sugar?" asked Eli, "No, first time I heard of it."

"Why am I not surprised?"

"You know very well how they control information here," said Enrique.

"Which is not to say that they don't try to control information where I come from. But here the control is total."

Eli asked, "What about what they always say here about how the multinationals control the governments in the U.S. and Europe? Is that true? And if so, does everyone know about that?"

"It's true, although I don't know if it's to the extent that they control the government. But there's no question that they have much influence on the government. It's kind of an institutional corruption and it's been going on much too long. And yes, everybody knows about it."

"Then why do the people put up with it?" asked Consuelo. "I mean being democracies and all."

"That's a good question, Consuelo. And I wish I knew the answer. But I guess it's because it's happened for so long that people have accepted it as the way of the world. Or maybe it's because, in democracies, it's not always the majority that rules, but those that make the most noise or have the most money to influence politicians. But there's something else. I think people don't fully appreciate the power of the vote and of capitalism itself, which is a way of voting with one's money. So they misuse both. Too many people don't bother to vote in the U.S. and take the stance that their vote is insignificant. Also, too many people don't buy things with the mindset that they can influence society through what they buy."

"I guess no political system is perfect," answered Consuelo.

"That's right, but at least in a democracy there is opportunity for change since the press is free. The press in the U.S. brought down a corrupt president and helped to end a terrible war. But in a country whose press represents the government and information is controlled, there's no chance of change. Let me give you an example: Have you ever heard of William Morgan, the Yankee Comandante?" None had. "Of course not. I'm sure he was erased from the official history of Cuba according to the Castros."

"The Yankee Comandante?" asked Ernesto, "You mean an American commander in the rebel army?"

"Right. William Morgan was one of two foreigners who gained the rank of *comandante* in the rebellion. The other one was Che Guevara. Morgan went into the Escambray Mountains (the mountain chain in central Cuba) and told the rebels he wanted to join because Batista had had his best friend tortured and murdered. He figured this would be more believable than telling them the truth: that he was just a soldier of fortune who wanted to fight for democratic principles against Batista. This was what all Cubans fought for before Che Guevara and Raúl Castro, two of the few real communists in the rebel army, asserted their influence in Fidel's quest for power. Because Morgan had been a Korean War veteran, he was already a well-trained soldier, unlike most men in the ragtag rebel army. At that first meeting, he impressed everyone when he threw a knife at a tree at 20 paces, nailing it right in the middle. He soon won their acceptance through skill and courage. Acceptance turned into admiration to the extent that he was given the highest rank in the rebel army and given command of the so-called Second Front of the Revolution. He learned to speak Spanish fluently in no time, which led to more respect. He even made time for romance; he fell in love with one of the rebel ladies, I forget her name, something Rodríguez, with whom he had two daughters."

"You never heard of this guy, Eli?" asked Enrique.

"You know what, I think I do remember hearing something about an American in the rebel army. But I never read about it anywhere; it was all hearsay."

"Of course not," I continued. "That's because Morgan embodied what went wrong with the Revolution. You may not be aware of this, but the fact is that in 1959 nobody suspected that Cuba would become a communist state. Like Morgan, we all thought we were fighting for democracy to return to Cuba and Fidel often assured us of this. Many historians believe that Fidel turned to communism only because it was the only way to retain power, that the Americans drove him to that because they acted on well-founded suspicions that there were communist influences behind the revolution."

"This is all news to me," said Enrique.

"You can imagine how betrayed many people felt. But back to Morgan. In '59 he saved Fidel's life when, acting as a double agent, he blew wide open a plot by Rafael Trujillo, the Dominican dictator, to assassinate Fidel. Morgan had duped the conspirators into believing that he wanted to kill Castro and he cooperated with them in appearance only while keeping Castro informed all the time. On the night that the conspirators landed their plane to start the operation, Castro and Morgan were waiting for them and killed them in a skirmish. So this added to Morgan's legendary reputation. But as the evidence mounted that Cuba was turning communist, Morgan began to express his disapproval and sense of betrayal of what he and his men had fought and many died for. In secret, he began to plot a counter-revolution, sending weapons to the Escambray, where other disaffected members of the old Second Front were gathering. Unfortunately, the plot was uncovered and Morgan was arrested. He was tried for treason and on trumped-up charges that he had been a triple agent for the CIA. They shot him the next day. The truth is that the real traitors were the communists, who betrayed the ideals for which everyone fought."

"This is all true, Gabriel?" asked Consuelo, sipping her rum then adding, "It sounds like a novel or a Hollywood story."

"All documented, Consuelo. But if you think what I told you so far sounds Hollywood, wait until you hear how he died. That night they marched him up to the wall before the firing squad, floodlights on him.

Someone behind the lights said, 'Kneel and beg for your life.' Morgan replied, 'I kneel for no man.' The voice whispered something and they shot him in the right knee. Morgan tried to keep standing, but got shot in the left knee and made to kneel before the final barrage."

"Hollywood should make a movie of his life," said Eli. "What a man, what *cojones!*"

"What *cojones* indeed," I echoed. "Maybe they *will* make a movie of him some day. They'd be fools not to."

After a warm farewell to Eli's friends, I had him take me back to Casa Nilma. Arriving at the front door, I told him that I had to go to El Vedado to be closer to the Ministry of External Affairs and the lawyer. Eli's face crumbled a bit: this meant I would not need his services any longer since *bicitaxis* can only function profitably in the short distances of the compact and crowded Old Havana. I gave him my address and phone number in Costa Rica and he gave me his address in Old Havana. I told him I'd come by before I went back to Costa Rica. He said, "that would make me happy. I love you, Gabriel."

"I love you too, Eli. Please take care and accept this little gift." I handed him 20 CUC's. His face wavered and then tears started to stream from his eyes. We hugged for a long moment and that was that.

When I opened the door the clock up at the "suite" was striking twenty. I could see some new guests or invitees had arrived. Yendri welcomed me as she was clearing dinner plates from the table and asked me if I was hungry. "Is the Pope German?" I answered.

She laughed her carefree laugh and said, "I take it that's a yes."

"Yes, Yendri, I'm starving, thank you." She left for the kitchen.

I sat down at the table to wait. Jaime sat at the other end talking to a swarthy kid in his early twenties. Again he gave me the wary eye, then he nodded at me, and so did the boy. I stood up, shook hands with Jaime and introduced myself to the young man, whose name was Geiner. Beyond the table at the balcony was a family watching the sunset. Nilma noticed my presence and came over and said, "Welcome, Gabriel! I want to introduce you to some people from your adopted country." She led me to the balcony, where I met Don Sebastian and the rest of his family, his wife Yolanda and his other son and the daughter, both still youngsters. They were from Cartago, Costa Rica, and were staying the night before going on to Varadero in the morning. Don Sebastian asked me where I lived in Costa Rica."

"I live in one of the most beautiful little towns in the world, Puerto Jiménez."

His eyes widened, "Jiménez! You don't say! Why we were just there last year for Easter. You're right. Beautiful little town. What a view that Golfo Dulce!"

"What a view indeed, Don Sebastian. I feel so lucky to live there. I suppose that's your son over there."

"Yes, Geiner. He's such a good student. He loves history and politics. That's why he's over there talking to Don Jaime."

We chatted on about Jiménez and Costa Rica and my background as a Cuban-American. As most people, he was happy that a foreigner appreciated his country and decided to live there. Then Yendri sang out, "Rafael, dinner is served!"

I sat down to eat at the other end of the table from Jaime and Geiner. The boy must have asked Jaime questions about Cuba or Latin American history because the *Granma* writer was lecturing him with the map of Latin America between them.

"...and here's the mountainous region of Bolivia where the CIA murdered Che Guevara after his valiant attempt to start our Revolution in Bolivia." As he said the word murdered, Jaime glanced my way. "Unfortunately, a traitor gave away his position in these mountains and he was cornered and captured. You wouldn't believe the last words of this glorious man. He was alone in this hut with the man who had been sent to kill him. He said to him, 'I know you've come to kill me. Shoot. Do it!' The man raised his rifle, but hesitated. Then Che's last words were, 'Shoot me, you coward! You are only going to kill a man!" Then the swine shot him several times until he expired."

"He was truly brave, Don Jaime."

"Yes, he was. One of the great men of the 20th century!"

"What about Venezuela? Why did they call it the Bolivarian Revolution? What did Simón Bolívar have to do with that revolution?"

"Raúl and Fidel counseled Hugo Chávez about this. Like José Martí, the great liberator of Cuba from imperialist Spain, Simón Bolívar was the great liberator of Latin America from the Spanish Crown. Both men believed the poor and the disadvantaged should rule and that

Latin America should have its own form of government different from North America. The Yankees are the new imperialists, so both great men would have been against them in the great struggle for sovereignty and independence from the yoke of the imperialist."

I finished my plate and took it to the kitchen for Yendri and Nilma before rejoining Don Sebastian and the rest of his family in the balcony. "Your son is a bright boy. He asks questions and good ones. How old is he?"

"He's 22, just finished his third year at the University of Costa Rica. We're very proud of him, if only these two lazy bones would imitate him," he said, pursing his lips at the youngsters. The two young ones looked around embarrassed.

"Well, they're still young. I'd give them a few years and they'll come around I'm sure. Right guys?" Both nodded, relieved.

"If you don't mind my asking, what is your profession?" asked Yolanda.

"I'm a teacher. Always have been," I said, adding in a low voice, "That's why I'm a little worried about your son."

"Why is that?" asked Sebastian.

"I couldn't help listening to the lecture he was getting from Jaime. Look, I don't know your political inclination, but let me ask you: You do realize you're in a communist totalitarian state, don't you?"

"Isn't that an exaggeration? I mean the people seem fine and they haven't rebelled since the Castros came to power."

This last remark I'd heard so many times in Costa Rica, as if it were a catch-all, end-all to negative conversations about Fidel Castro—if Fidel were so bad, why has he remained in power for so long? In other words, the great length of his dictatorship means he must be benevolent. So I said, "The length of time in power of a dictator is no indication of his benevolence, Don Sebastian. In fact, I'd say it's more likely a sign of his cunning and ruthlessness. Saddam Hussein was in power 30 years. Joseph Stalin, who murdered over 20 million of his countrymen, died of natural causes in power after over 30 years. Mao, who did away with at least 50 million Chinese, also died of old age in power."

"I didn't know these men had killed so many and were so long in power. But if they were, of course you're right. But I don't think you can put the Castros in the same group as these men you mentioned."

"I agree with you, they're not in the same category of egregious-ness, but my real point is that they are communists and the communists are well known for complete control of education and information, especially manipulating and distorting information, and your son is getting the party line at the table right now."

"Really? What's he saying to him?"

"Well, for instance, I overheard Jaime say that the CIA murdered El Che. In fact, they tried to save him, but the dictator of Bolivia at that time, I forget his name, didn't want his capture and trial to become Che's showcase for the Bolivian's own terrible governance, so he had him executed over the objections of the CIA, who wanted him for inter-rogation."

"Really? I also thought the CIA murdered him. You're not giving me the Yankee party line?"

I smiled replying, "One thing you can be sure of, Sebastian, in the U.S. or for that matter, most of Europe, you can get both sides of any ideology. But frankly, Don Sebastian, it doesn't surprise me—I mean your doubting my words. Look I've lived in Costa Rica long enough to know that what they teach your children is much influenced by the Castros' version of history. Costa Rica is after all a socialist state, a nice mixture of socialism and capitalism, but ideologically, it's pretty social-ist."

"You know very well, Gabriel. What else did he say?"

"That Simón Bolívar and José Martí would have supported the Cuban and the Bolivarian Revolutions."

"That's not true?"

"Of course not. Both men were admirers of the American Revo-lution and its principles. They also admired American society and its meritocracy." He looked at me doubtfully. "Look, Simón Bolívar was a Freemason and a child of the Creole oligarchy. Not exactly the back-ground for a socialist. Both he and Martí believed in fairness and equal-ity for the poor and freedom from Spanish colonialism, but both were essentially liberal democrats, not totalitarian dictators and least of all communists. Bolívar died when Marx was a boy, so how would he have approved of something that hadn't even been thought of yet? In fact, I remember reading that Marx wrote a biography of Simón Bolívar and, if I remember correctly, he had nothing but disdain for him!"

We continued this back and forth for a while, Sebastian challenging my assertions and I defending them, when Jaime, Nilma, Yendri and Geiner showed up at the entrance to the balcony.

"Intelligent boy you have here, Sebastian," said Jaime, "I'm sure he's a brilliant student at university."

"He's not bad. But don't put any ideas in his head."

"What do you mean, Sebastian?" said Jaime, a guilty look on his face.

"I don't want him to get a big head. Worst thing for a kid."

Jaime, looking relieved, said, "I see. You're right, but this boy is humble. I wouldn't worry. Listen, we have to say goodnight. It's been a pleasure."

The two groups bid goodnight and I was left alone with the Costa Rican family in the balcony.

Sebastian said, "Sit down, Geiner, we were just talking about your chat with Jaime."

"Yes, I couldn't help hearing your conversation while I was having dinner. I was telling your father a little about it, I mean what I heard Jaime tell you."

"Yes, son, what did you think about what he told you?" asked Yolanda.

"Most of it was crap," said Geiner.

Alone in bed that night. I recalled an old Mark Twain anecdote that went something like this: "Back when I was a boy of 18 I thought my old man was a complete idiot. Then I went away to school and came back home four years later. After talking to him for a while, I was amazed to discover how much the old man had learned in four years!"

Smiling at this clever anecdote, I thought of Geiner's response to his mother's question, which was the last thing we expected from the young man. We had all laughed aloud when he said it. Geiner had not only caught up to his old man, he had surpassed him. The boy had cut through and studied his history well, beyond the propaganda, by relying on something his father had not had, the Internet. Geiner ended up backing just about everything I had told his father, except he didn't know about Marx's biography and his disdain for Simón Bolívar, but it didn't surprise Geiner, knowing what he knew about Bolívar, who wasn't perfection on Earth either. The boy had even agreed with me about El Che's specious accomplishments and greatness—he understood his flaw as a fanatic prone to violence as his tool of persuasion. Then he added: "And Don Jaime didn't seem to see that the man he called a traitor for betraying Che's position was really a patriot to his own country. The man was a Bolivian, after all. Besides, what Che was doing in Bolivia was what the Cubans are always accusing the Americans of: trying to overthrow the government of a Latin country, which, of course, the Americans did, but it's not like they were the only ones. This is how the Cold War was waged."

Yolanda and Sebastian wound up convinced I was right because of Geiner's corroboration. Because of the experience, they grew even prouder of their brilliant son. Sebastian had asked Geiner, "Didn't you challenge him?"

He'd replied, "It wouldn't have made any difference. I just wanted to confirm the crap that's fed to the Venezuelan and Cuban people. And that guy's an expert in crap. I have a friend who went to study in Venezuela and he told me there it's getting quite bad, and it's looking a lot like Cuba. Long lines to buy anything. Free press eliminated. Silencing of the political opposition."

In one way, though, Geiner's take and stance didn't surprise me but in another way, it did. It didn't surprise me in that one of the things that's different about the new generation, something much influenced by the Internet, is that they can supplant their parent's generation in knowledge and theory and sometimes in know-how *within the lifetime of their parents*, a modern phenomenon. In Mark Twain's era, the parents always outpaced their offspring in knowledge. No wonder the Chinese, North Koreans and Cubans fear the Internet and jam or block out unsympathetic news, Websites or information; they don't want anyone to get ahead of them in information and there is information that is just plain forbidden. Clearly, Geiner was way ahead of his parents, at least in the specialty of history and politics.

On the other hand, it surprised me because Costa Rica is a socialist state that plays by the rules of capitalism. Its ideology is quite a bit left of center and so is the educational content of the social studies courses for its youth. I've read some high school texts where they laud the Cuban Revolution as a victory over the imperialist oppressors, yet there's not a peep about the totalitarian state that runs Cuba, and its human rights violations. Most people take what they have been brought up with as gospel without ever reassessing later in life what they have been taught. That leftist schooling brought up Geiner's parents and Geiner himself, but to his credit, he had overcome it in his own pursuit of truth as a young scholar.

The whole experience evoked in me the memory of a line from Wordsworth's poem, *The Rainbow*: "The child is father of the man." It was meant to suggest that the man results from the child and, therefore, the child is his father. But here I witnessed a brilliant boy who had put a twist to the great saying, for he had succeeded in changing his father's political view of the world and in a way behaved like—literally become—a father to his own father.

Geiner and I exchanged e-mails and promised to write after the trip, a promise we both have kept.

I wrote everything down and went to sleep with a tendency to smile.

DAY SIX

The Colombians woke me. They had just returned from Varadero and were checking in before returning to Colombia the next day. I noticed right away they all looked haggard and pale. I asked them how they liked Varadero.

"A nice beach," one said, "but too bad about the food and the service. Both the worst we've ever experienced."

"Two of us got sick from the food and I think everybody has diarrhea," said another. Can't recommend it."

"Tell me about it," I said. "The only good food I've had here was in a privately owned restaurant and right here at Casa Nilma."

I packed, paid Nilma and asked for a cab. Ana came in to say goodbye, ever with those two contradictory expressions on her face: the smile of her mouth and the strained sadness of her eyes. I had prepared for the moment, inserting a 20 CUC bill in her hand as I kissed her goodbye. Kissing her cheek, I whispered, "This is for your son's camera. Good luck." She pressed together her trembling lips and assented with her eyes now tearing. Her lips mimed, "*Gracias, gracias.*"

Because Ramón, Yendri's taxi driver husband was busy, they had called their alternate chauffeur. "Do you know where Casa Sandra is in El Vedado, sir?" I asked the bald heavy-set man behind the wheel of a navy blue 1958 Buick.

"Casa Sandra? Not only do I know where it is, they're good friends of mine, Sandra and Silvio, great people."

He drove on, taking the avenue along the Malecón west toward El Vedado, the blue open Caribbean seething off to our right, the hotels and ministries scraping the blue to the left. I asked him what I had been asking all Cubans I caught alone: "What do you think of life in Cuba?"

Without fail, Vladimir embarked on the litany of complaints, beginning with the phrase, "Unadorned shit." He continued with the usual grievances I'd heard before, but then he commented on something I'd wondered about all along: what percentage of Cubans really support the revolution?

"The thing is," he began, "there are three types of Cubans: you have the Communist Party Line type, the Dissenters and then the vast majority that I call the Pretenders. The Party Line type is maybe 15, 25 percent of the population; these are the die-hard communists that really believe in the shit that they've been fed since birth. They're the best off economically and they profit from all the favoritism the regime offers them. The Dissenters are people that openly disagree with the Revolution and try to change things. They are ostracized, harassed, often lose their jobs, many are in prison and if not, they often manage to live through charity or underground work; I would estimate this group is 10, 15 percent tops. Then you have the majority, which is maybe 50 to 60 percent of the population, that only to their most trusted individuals express their real feelings, but publicly are gung-ho communists. They spend their life pretending because if not, things would not be too pleasant. Yes, indeed, we've become a country of pretenders."

I told him the story of Gretel, the engineer turned prostitute who had left El Montserrate through the back door to avoid being picked up.

"Typical," he said. "She would have been charged with what they call *peligrosidad* (dangerousness) to the Revolution. They don't want anyone talking too long to foreigners, especially a Cuban-American like you, because they get firsthand knowledge of what it's like on the outside. They're afraid that you will 'corrupt' them. And, by the way, keep your eyes peeled because you can be sure you're being watched or followed. That cop that was watching her probably had been following you."

"You know I wondered about that too. You really think so?"

"Let me ask you: Since you've been here, have you said anything against the Revolution in front of a group of people?" I told him about my argument about the embargo with Jaime. "That's it. You can count on it. Keep your mouth shut while you're here."

After he'd finished spilling the beans on the revolution, he suddenly said, "You know, Sandra and Silvio are very nice people, the best, but they're die-hard communists. Just so you know."

"Thanks for telling me. I'll keep it in mind." Then it occurred to me that not only can one be a communist and be a really good person, but most communists, especially those not in power, are excellent, idealistic people who often represent the best in humanity. For at the heart of communism resides the desire for everyone to be equal (the removal of the class struggle) and the primacy of everyone helping and supporting each other, both moral and rational concepts. The former tries to eliminate capitalism's social inequality, its hollow materialism, and the nagging and irrational feeling that one doesn't quite measure up without money and possessions. And the latter, well isn't it one of the fundamental messages of Christ? So there is nothing wrong with the ideas underlying communism. But as most people know by now, it doesn't work because it demands perfection from humanity's imperfection.

Any system that refuses to work with human nature is doomed unless sustained through fear and subterfuge. What has happened in all instances of the implementation of communism? Following the honeymoon of "the revolution" comes the realization by those in power that many refuse to toe the line. The remedy? As it happened in Cuba, to force conformity through four methods:

> (1) The massive subornation of the underclass through subsidies in housing, education, guaranteed employment and health, also done to morally disarm the people. (2) The execution, exile or imprisonment of the opposition, usually the educated class. (3) The elimination of a free and independent press. (4) The establishment of a mandatory and prescriptive education system with the emphasis on *what* to think instead of *how* to think.

My new hosts, Sandra and Silvio, I would discover, were unwitting victims of especially the last method.

Casa Sandra turned out to be an apartment, where the couple lived, with an adjacent room with a private bathroom. These dwellings were part of a large manor that had been subdivided. Sandra and Silvio expected me since I had made arrangements days earlier. I knocked on the door and both septuagenarians, faces beaming, appeared and filled the doorframe as it opened from left to right. I could tell Sandra had once been a beauty with classic Mediterranean features now blurred with age. Betraying a remnant of vanity, her hair was dyed black. Silvio was older, perhaps nearing 80, with gray close-cropped hair, blue eyes bulging behind thick glasses. "Welcome, *compañero*," said Sandra, "Yes, welcome to our home," said Silvio, "Please come in and sit down."

Sandra and I sat while Silvio went off to the kitchen beyond the living room. "Since you're Cuban I suspect you won't object to a little rum and juice, right?" Silvio said at the sound of ice dropping in glasses.

"You guessed it, don Silvio." Sandra and I exchanged pleasantries. "The last time I was in Cuba was fifty years ago, everyone called each other *camarada*. Now, it's *compañero*. When did that change?"

"Oh years ago, I guess. I suppose it sounded too Russian to many people at some point." *Compañero* sounds to me much more Latin, don't you think?"

"Absolutely. I never liked *comrade* for that reason. Not really Cuban."

When Silvio came back with three rum and peach juice cocktails, I was telling Sandra about getting the birth certificate. Silvio handed them out and sat down next to me. We toasted and drank. Then Sandra said, "You must have been a boy when you left, do you remember much about Cuba from those days?"

"Actually, now that I'm back, it surprises me how much I do remember." And that is where the conversation about my past in Cuba ended. They never pressed me about what I remembered, why my family left or under what circumstances. They were either not interested or afraid of stirring an impasse. I suspected it was for the latter.

"You know, so much has happened since you left," said Silvio. "Many changes, many advancements. In medicine, the health of the people, education. We eradicated many diseases and literacy now is nearly 100 percent!"

"Yes, no question about that, don Silvio. I'm very impressed at how well educated most Cubans seem. It has been a great accomplishment of the Revolution."

"Yes, sir, it has," Silvio went on, encouraged at the first sign of my political compliance. "But you know what, some changes will surprise even the most liberal communists and those changes have been good too."

"Really? Like what Silvio?"

"Well, like that now they're going to let people leave the island

and travel abroad, and people can buy and sell homes and cars and you can start your own business as long as it's small. Why four blocks away there's a great restaurant called La Pachanga that serves food like the old days before the Revolution. It's privately owned so the owner really cares about the quality of the food and you can really taste the difference. The only thing is they should have done these things 40 years ago!"

I couldn't believe my ears. Every "privilege" he marveled at was an old-hat right outside the island. Here was a man telling me about the great recent changes of the Revolution and he had no idea or chose to ignore that they were concessions to capitalism. Furthermore, it appeared he had no hard feelings it had taken over 40 years for the Castro brothers to realize these no-brainer improvements, which had been the proper thing to do all along and that he and the whole nation had had to live without them for their entire lives! Just then I resisted a very strong urge to tell Silvio what I felt. For I thought, "Who am I to ruin the illusions of a nice old couple near the end of their lives? Were my arguments and ideas so damn sacrosanct that they were worth instilling doubt in the lives of a good pair of old communists?" No, I decided.

So I stayed shallow. "You know, Silvio, the next day after I arrived here I ordered a Cuban sandwich from a state run restaurant and it was the worst sandwich I ever had. You're telling me I can finally have the sandwich of my dreams?"

Alone in the rented room after Sandra had left, I stood and looked around. The room's only window faced the corridor whose line of windows across the hall outside the room provided the only natural light. There was a 21-inch TV below the window. A floor fan from some Central European country stood in front of the queen-size bed with night tables and lamps on either side. An antique mahogany commode with a glass top straddled the corner. There were many photos under the glass, some of children, some of the elderly, some of youths in the flush of life. A beautiful woman with classic Mediterranean lines smiled through the radiance of youth. "Sandra in her twenties," I said to myself. Next to her stared a handsome square-jawed youth sporting a military mustache. He was in the Cuban Army's olive green uniform. His jaw set below the mustache, he appeared to thrust forward the arm with the black and red July 26th Movement armband, the flag of the revolutionary army. In his eyes was a mix of arrogance and defiance. It was reminiscent of the I-dare-you-to-knock-it-off gesture of adolescents. "And Silvio in his late teens," I said aloud and shook my head thinking, "I guess they got to him pretty early." I took a shower, turned on the fan and the TV and got in bed. The news show was a half-hour of good news: agricultural accomplishments in rural Cuba, an anticholera vaccination drive, the upcoming visit by the Chinese prime minister, Raúl's speech at the National Assembly. No murders, no thefts, no rapes, no drug arrests. A never-never land of perfection. It made me so sleepy I decided to take a siesta, partly to recharge my batteries, partly to be unconscious during the worst of Havana's summer midday heat. As I faded away though, my mind wandered to a day back in 1960 when I was with my old man watching television on a channel long since gone...

"Something smells fishy here," declared my father in front of his friends at the Liceo Social Club in Holguín. They had been half-listening to Che Guevara's speech on television, but my father, with the lawyer's nose for oratory, had been listening intently and what he had just heard stank. Guevara had declared that "any holdings over 3,300 acres were to be expropriated by the government and either redistributed to peasants in 67-acre parcels or held as state-run communes."

"What do you mean, Facundo?" asked one of the friends.

"I mean this smells red! Didn't you hear? They're going to take land away from people!"

"Yes, Cundo, but they will surely compensate the owners! Hey, this is for the good of all."

"Compensation? He said nothing about compensation! This now, then what?"

"Come now, *chico*, they'll surely compensate. It's natural."

"Well I guess we'll soon find out," said my father, who had nothing to lose by the new agrarian reform law, for his land, inherited from his father, was 2,800 acres. But he was right: there would be no compensation. Later he would regret his outburst in front of his friends as well as his tendency to express his misgivings about the Revolution, for there came a time when he was no longer sure who was his friend and he'd become a suspected counter-revolutionary. The rude late-night, four-note rappings at the door became frequent. On a few occasions they took him away and he didn't come home until the wee hours. A capable lawyer, he knew how to defend himself under interrogation, knew when a question would lead him to a trap. And so he always managed to return home. Nevertheless, the harassment continued.

Then one day not long after the Second Agrarian Reform, father received a letter informing him that the farm that his father had forged from will and sweat was no longer his. This he accepted with the fatality born of prison or death. "Consuelo," he said to mother as my brother, Facundito, and I listened, "It's clear this is no longer the country we were born in. We have to leave."

By six I was walking with my camera for El Malecón. The sunset was still over two hours away and I wanted to experience and get some shots of one of the world's most famous promenades. I took a *colectivo* up to the street where I had been left off to walk to the Ministry of External Affairs three days ago and about a kilometer later the vista opened up before me in all its grandeur, a broad sweeping half-moon bay, miles either way, the Caribbean's white-capped waves dropping off into the horizon. A light breeze blowing in, the air smelled of the sea. To the right in the distance was Morro Castle. I crossed the six-lane two-way boulevard and sat on the seawall facing the great city. A hodgepodge of buildings lined the boulevard. Some were grand sky-scrapers, some, dilapidated manors that once housed the rich, some, stone husks in disrepair. I stood and walked towards the castle.

A square six-story building of the form-follows-function archi-tecture of the 50's loomed up on the other side of the boulevard. It only caught my eye because rows of dozens of black flags with a white star flapped on poles set at differing heights in front of the building. I crossed the boulevard over to a sidewalk bar where there were two barkeeps in their thirties and ordered a mojito. "I'll make you one of the best mojitos you'll ever have!" said the older of the two, a white man with piercing green eyes. With flair, he mixed the drink before me, while the other bartender looked on amused, as if he'd seen this all before. Finished, he said, "Here it is. Manuel's Mojito, extra strong, for the entertainment of your palate." With exaggerated reverence, I picked up the cocktail, scrutinized its appearance and took a good long draft.

"Manuel, you're no bartender," I deadpanned. Manuel's eyebrows furred with concern. "You're a magician!" Manuel let out a chuckle.

"Thanks! You had me going. Didn't I tell you? Where are you from? Your accent is kind of Cuban, but then not quite."

"It's a long story. But I'm from here, born here, but my family left long ago because of the Revolution." His eyes flicked right and left before he answered.

"I see. You from Miami?"

"Started in Miami, but my family wound up in Chicago. I introduced myself extending my hand.

"Manuel. This is Ivan." We shook hands with the customary strong grip of Cubans.

"Manuel, please make yourselves a mojito on me. A man should never drink alone, right?" For an instant, I saw fireworks in their eyes.

"That's right, for God's sake!" said Ivan.

Manuel mixing the cocktails, I asked, "What's with all those black flags in front of that building?"

"Oh, that's the U.S. Embassy," replied Ivan, "The black flags are meant to piss off the Yankees."

Manuel added, "It's not really an embassy; what's it called ... an interests office, or something like that. The building is really the Swiss Embassy and they rent part of it to the States. Yes, the whole thing started when the office began running Christmas messages on an electronic billboard on the top floor. The government is atheist and they didn't like the messages, so they put up all those flags to hide them." He finished the mojitos. I raised mine and said, "*Salud*, gentlemen."

"*Salud!*" they chorused. We drank deeply, polishing them off in no time. "Another round, Manuel!" They loosened up with the drinks. We small talked a while. I took their pictures. Manuel went to the bar's inner courtyard full of tables full of people. Ivan asked me how much I'd paid for the camera. I told him and asked if cameras like these were sold in Cuba. He said no, no one has the money to buy them so they don't even try to sell them. I told him about Ana and her dream of get-

The U.S. Interests Section with the black flags flapping in front. They were erected to block the view of the electronic billboard that ran at the top of the building. The Interests Section would run messages like the George Burns quote, "How sad that all the people who would know how to run this country are driving taxis or cutting hair." Today the flags are gone and the Stars and Stripes wave from the same breeze.

ting a camera like this for her son. Ivan looked down then said, "We don't have many freedoms here in Cuba." Manuel came back excited for some reason. "Hey, Gabriel, you like girls, right?"

"Of course I like girls, what do you take me for?"

"I'll be back!" Manuel swerved back into the courtyard and returned a minute later. "OK, she's coming in a moment. You would not believe this girl, she's a bonbon. Twenty-five CUC should do. You'll love her!" Before I could object, the girl was coming. A white girl in her late teens approached as if she were walking on a tightrope of lilies. That cushiony flesh of youth clung to her exuberance. Manuel said, "This is Yoany. What do you think?"

"It would be difficult for you to be more beautiful, Yoany."

"Thank you," Yoany said lowering her eyelids, smiling radiantly, then opening her piercing green eyes and peering straight into mine. Manuel stood back a bit just then, although not as far back as I would have liked, as Ivan went off into the courtyard. I looked at Manuel then back at Yoany. Manuel looked away.

"Incredible," I muttered. "Manuel, would you give us a minute, please?" Manuel said of course and ambled away to the far end of the bar. I looked into Yoany's eyes and said, "Look Yoany, Manuel never consulted me before he brought you here. If he had, I would have told him I wasn't interested." She looked a little hurt just then and I added, "Not because I don't find you attractive, but because I'm not that kind of man. It's hard for me to be impersonal with sex." She looked down as if embarrassed, but I pressed on. "I also don't like that your own brother is playing the role of your pimp." She looked up, breathed hard then looked down again. "He *is* your brother, isn't he?" She nodded still looking down. I took out enough to cover the mojitos, put it on the counter, and walked away, Manuel calling out my name behind me.

As I walked across the boulevard back to the Malecón, my mind was reeling. I asked myself what could drive a brother to turn into his younger sister's pimp. The reason is, of course, humanity's greatest villain: poverty. Poverty often makes people do things that compromise their dignity and integrity; it first weakens then corrupts them. One of the proudest accomplishments of the Revolution was that it eliminated the gambling and prostitution that had plagued Havana as the American mafia had bought off the Batista regime to turn the capital into the playground of the "imperialist Yankees." Batista had ensured that anybody with the ready cash to invest in a hotel or casino would be fast-tracked for a license without the normal red tape as long as the dictator got 10 to 30 percent of the income. Meyer Lansky and Lucky Luciano became beneficiaries of Batista's "largesse." The fed up population ransacked the hotels and casinos as the rebels approached the capital in the wee hours of January 1, 1959, and the hated dictator fled the island for Spain, taking with him $40 million. Left behind were an estimated 100,000 soon to be unemployed prostitutes. And so they remained for a long time.

Following the fall of the Soviet Union, however, what Castro called "The Special Period" began. The rug of sugar and petroleum subsidies was suddenly pulled from under the regime. It didn't help that the U.S. ratcheted up the embargo forbidding ships that had done trade with Cuba to berth at U.S. ports for six months. Deprived of the old subsidies and trade with the Eastern Bloc, real hunger plagued the island in the early to mid 90's. The kind of hunger that compels you to eat grass and tree bark. Animals disappeared from zoos overnight, as did much of the cat population. The reality that the real world runs on capitalist principles settled in the mind of the aging dictator. The Soviet honeymoon was over and Cuba for the first time since the Revolution had to fend for itself. Castro did the only thing he could: turn capitalist at least at the state level. The choice of industry for his new campaign had been under his nose for decades: Cuba, with its beautiful music and dance, white sand beaches, tropical weather and colonial architecture is a tourism paradise. Thus began in 1995 a massive effort to develop the tourism industry. But since Cuba was broke, Fidel encouraged foreign investment, essentially what Batista had done. There is, however, a difference: What some have called the "tourism apartheid" was instituted. Cubans are not allowed in tourist-designated facilities unless they work there and they are not allowed to have dollars. In order to get a job in the tourist industry, however, you must have a proven track record as a staunch member of the Cuban Communist Party—if you're going to be talking to foreigners every day, the regime wants to be sure you will speak well of the regime; this is the main reason I have so often heard visitors to the island assure me that the people of Cuba are completely happy with the regime—of course, they have only been in the tourist centers and have talked only to the island's most rabid communists.[1]

At any rate, in the late 1990's Cuba opened herself to the world for the first time since 1959 and prostitution returned with a vengeance. At the heart of the problem is that people whose average income is 15 to 20 dollars a month become susceptible to the sex tourism industry. Prostitutes, or *jineteras* (female jockeys) that on average would sell their bodies for 100 euros in Europe do so for 20 or less in Cuba. Eli had told me that child prostitution has turned into a family affair with parents pimping their daughters for spare cash. As a result, we have come full circle with respect to prostitution in Cuba, the difference being that there are likely many more prostitutes today per capita than when Cuba was known as "the brothel of the Caribbean." One great and telling irony, however, is that the price of a prostitute has remained the same since the 1950's, an indication the Cuban economy has been essentially stagnant for half a century. Another is that, as Castro himself once acknowledged: "One day when I was down in Brazil, an Argentinian asked me 'Is it true that some girls who are university graduates sometimes practice prostitution?' I replied instantly, without thinking, 'That proves prostitutes in Cuba have a university level.'"[2]

Castro may have been half-joking and half-pointing with pride at Cuba's achievements in education, but the anecdote inadvertently underscored a disturbing paradox: What is the point of a higher education if at the end of it, the best you can do is to put it all aside and sell your body to make a real living?

I soon came upon the Monument to the *Maine*, two stalwart ionic columns standing side by side. Gone long ago, torn down in 1961 following the Bay of Pigs invasion, was the three-ton bronze American eagle that perched, one claw on each capital, her spread wings facing the Caribbean north, symbolizing America's promise to "fly home"

The Monument to the *Maine* today. The American Eagle that straddled the capitals of the columns was torn down after the 1961 Bay of Pigs debacle.

after helping Cuba gain independence. Inscribed near the base is the regime's historical take on the ill-fated battleship, whose explosion, killing 266 U.S. sailors, was the pretext for the U.S. to enter Cuba's war of independence against Spain: *To the victims of the Maine who were sacrificed by the imperialists' voracity and their desire to gain control of the island of Cuba. February 1898–February 1961.* The new dedication, refers to the conspiracy theory that the U.S. sabotaged the *Maine*, blamed the Spanish and entered the war of independence in order to wrest from the mother country her last colonies—Cuba, the Philippines, Puerto Rico and Guam. Most historians agree that the explosion was the result of an internal mechanical problem that had caused nearby stored gunpowder and munitions to blow up. No evidence of a conspiracy has ever been found. There is no question, however, that the U.S. government and the yellow press led by William Randolph Hearst jumped on the tragedy implying that it was an act of Spanish sabotage and thus the U.S. had a pretext to enter the war. Yet the fact that the regime has elected a baseless conspiracy theory as an official historical fact points to the lengths it goes to in order to support its stance that the U.S. as a greedy imperialist monster who will stop at nothing.

Then a little farther on perched on a low hill I beheld one of the grandest of Havana's landmarks, the Hotel Nacional, an eight-story cross-shaped neocolonialist gem built in the 30's. As it has been well cared for, it looked the same as when I had left 50 years before. I thought about the list of guests I remembered reading about God knows when, good names like Frank Sinatra, Ava Gardner, Mickey Mantle, Johnny Weissmuller, Rocky Marciano, Errol Flynn, John Wayne, Marlene Dietrich, Gary Cooper, Marlon Brando and, of course, Ernest Hemingway, but also bad names like Meyer Lansky, Frank Costello and Vito Genovese.

The latter all stayed and conferred there to mull their gambling and prostitution plans for Cuba—the conference dramatized in *The Godfather Part II* wherein the gang, on the rooftop of the hotel, symbolically carved up Lansky's birthday cake topped with the map of Cuba. I took some shots of the grand old ghost house and moved on.

The closer to the Old Havana section of the promenade the more people milled about the seawall, some fishing in the high tide, others

"The Grand Old Ghost House," El Hotel Nacional.

using the wall to jump and swim in the sea, others singing and playing musical instruments, still others, lovers in embrace. But most were walking or conversing as they sat on the wall or walked along it in small groups. I approached a teenager who was with three cute little girls of mixed race. They looked like siblings. "Can I take your picture?" I asked the young woman. Before she could answer the three young ones started jumping up and down and one screamed, "Yes, let's do it, Carmen. Come on!" Then all three arranged themselves around the older sister in provocative poses like models on a beach. After each shot, they rearranged themselves for the next one. Between chuckles I showed them the shots on playback, thanked them and went on.

People, white, black and mulatto, streamed by, not separated by race but by groups. In Cuba, there seems to be no racial segregation. In all appearances, it is a colorless society, far more integrated than before the Revolution. Most of the half-million or so Cubans of the first exodus in the 60's were white. Like so many societies were at the time in Latin America, Cuba's was very racist. But could it be that a communist totalitarian state engenders racial equality? Maybe so. Although throughout the world what people have in common vastly outnumbers their differences, they irrationally latch on to their differences because of the ancient tug of tribalism. Humanity, after all, spent the bulk of its 200,000 years in a tribal state. Therefore, tribalism is in our genetic makeup (if you don't believe me, ask a fan of the Chicago

"Can I take your picture?" The four sisters on the Malecón, a testament to the insouciant charm of Cubans.

Cubs why he persists in cheering for his team; whatever he tells you, it's sure to be irrational and if he tells you that it's because he lives in the North Side, then you know it's because of tribalism—and *tribalism in today's world is irrational*). Race and class are two of the many differences (language, religion, culture and form of dress are others) that humanity seeks in order to hark back to the old "us vs. them." It is something beneath our skin and it moves us from within. Witness that the rich seek their own for friendship and the same goes for the middle class, although most wish they had a rich friend. The poor, of course, are always trying to find someone richer for a friend, but are met with all the barriers of class access. In America, the black poor population is still disproportionately large, which engenders a natural segregation, perhaps influenced as much by racism as by class difference. But in a generally classless society like Cuba's, whatever tribal barriers exist must be pretty weak.

I came up on a few guys fishing off the Malecón and snapped some photos. One of them, a big burly mulatto, looked up at me and said, "Ah, you're German, aren't you?"

"Wrong. Guess again."

"Let me guess, you're English!"

"No, you'll never guess."

"OK, OK, not with that accent. I know. You're CIA. That's it! You're a CIA man!"

"You got me," I said and walked away feeling very much like a neo-Alec Guinness in *Our Man in Havana* as he kept shouting to his friends, "Hey, guys! There goes a real CIA man! Hey, CIA Man!"

Going past a street that turned off the Malecón Boulevard, I saw an amazing sight rarely seen in America or for that matter anywhere else in the modern world: a street full of people of all ages playing in a variety of games. It was as if everyone that lived on that street were outside interacting, for the street was teeming with people. There were old and middle-aged men playing dominoes four at a time on plastic tables; some were playing chess. Little children played hide-and-seek. Boys lagged coins off building walls. Girls played jacks on doorsteps or hopscotch or jumped twirling ropes on the sidewalks like the girls do in Harlem. Boys played stickball, using broom handles for bats and tennis balls for baseballs, or soccer, using the gaps between opposing building columns as goals. Women playing cards. Old men and women sat, conversing and watching the young. People played all the old simple games. I stood on the corner, took some shots and gaped at the scene.

What a contrast was this spectacle, I thought, to the alienation of the modern world: a world of interaction through the intermediacy of machines, of lonely video games, and a family estranged from itself, a TV in every room, staring at the mindless 1000-channel crap, a world of text messages instead of real conversations, superficial "friends on Facebook," the "30 second sound bites," 148 symbol "twitters," and Instagrams, of the relentless bombardment of advertisements, overwhelming information, the breakneck speed of change, of planned obsolescence, the eternal "upgrade" and the mad insistence on the new, the trendy—whole maelstroms of distraction from what is important: ourselves and the beings that accompany us in the voyage of life. Here in this street before me was humanity in its essence; the way humans have been at leisure for the majority of their existence. "We have lost our way," I muttered. "This is how we were meant to be."

No matter what the intent behind this result, I had to admit this street was good and wonderful. As a Cuban friend in Costa Rica, who had lived much of her life in Cuba, said once to me after listening to my ravings about the generalized poverty of Cuba, "But, Gabriel, you know, they don't have much, but they rely on each other and take care of each other more. For example, if I didn't have a blouse that went with a skirt, I'd borrow one from a friend and she would borrow something from me when she needed it. So people are more together." The truth is that Cubans today are poor yes, but they're not starving or extreme poverty poor. They do without most of the comfort and convenience and "stuff" of our gotta-have-it-now consumer society. They don't have all those machines that come between us. Instead, they have each other. And the people I saw on that street with the golden light shining down on them were happy and lost in the sheer essence of their humanity.

But on the other hand, you have to wonder if this is the intended effect of the Revolution or an unintentional by-product. Maybe both. The Internet and e-mail are available to only trusted members of the Communist Party. Cell phones yes, but smart phones no. They do not exist since they require Internet connections. No X-Boxes or video games; no one has the money to buy them. Television is as much a propaganda tool as a means of entertainment. So does the regime maintain the salaries at absurdly low world levels in order to protect the people from "the intermediacy of machines"? Is the generalized poverty an instrument of forcing people to avoid the alienation of modern societies and experience the "essence of their humanity"? I doubt it. It is, rather, part the product of an absurd and corrupt command economy and part the need in such a system to control, invent or manipulate information for its survival. The regime, however, does its best through education to instill a sense of community. In fact, a sense of community is part and parcel of a communist state's theoretical end. For according to Marx, the goal of a communist state is not communism but a sort of democratic anarchy. And for anarchy to function, a sense of community is indispensable.

A reason for the failure of communism is that, as Marx prescribed, it must begin with the dictatorship of the proletariat. (Marx never expressed exactly how communism would work as an economic system nor established its "operating rules." Instead, his discourse was mainly the theory and the desired end result. The implementation and practice of communism have been, therefore, a matter of interpretation. Unfortunately, the first such interpretation turned into Stalinism, the dastardly foundation of 20th century "communism.") According to Marx, the state would naturally "wither away" in time and the people would then take charge and rule themselves *democratically*, guided by a shared societal good.[3] The end result would be this democratic anarchy, or a democratic absence of government, a political ideology that stands on two pillars: Humanity is fundamentally good, and humanity must be well-educated and, therefore, imbued with common sense and a sense of community. One of the reasons for the necessity of a period of total dictatorship is that a universal high level of education must be imposed on the people. The only problem is that absolute power, as the proverb goes, corrupts absolutely and, without the accountability engendered by a free vote and press, totalitarian dictatorships tend never to surrender power. The only instance of the state's ever withering away in the history of communism was that of the Soviet Union in 1989. But, instead of a democratic anarchy, it turned into a fledgling capitalist democracy.

Marx's dictum of the necessity of a dictatorship to jump start a communist state still has a hold on the neo-communist movements now being implemented in Latin America. As we witness the events in Venezuela since 1999 when Hugo Chávez was elected president, the government has focused on the incremental establishment of a totalitarian dictatorship, now nearly complete. In Rafael Correa's Ecuador, Evo Morales' Bolivia, and Cristina Kitchener's Argentina the elected governments are attempting to manacle or shut down the press and may be on their way to full-fledged dictatorships.

No. Marx was wrong about the state "withering away." The state in Cuba, after achieving enviable literacy levels, after two generations of thorough command of the educational system, domination of the media and the pounding of the moral motive for production, has not withered away. Rather, it depends on all those instruments to self-perpetuate.

And what of that wonderful street scene out of days gone by? Well, that was beautiful, but in the end I had to come down to earth and to admit: It's what people do in today's world when they have nothing else to do. It's what people do in Sub-Saharan Africa for entertainment. My conclusion was easy. In the U.S., if I don't want to listen to a commercial, I have the freedom to turn it off; if I don't want to use Facebook or Twitter, no one forces me to get an account; if I want my child to play real instead of virtual games, I can have that too; if I don't want to associate with people who only converse through a machine, that is also my prerogative—although that's a long shot in today's Western society. But in a totalitarian state or in an impoverished society one doesn't have any choice but to be like the people in that street in Havana.

I walked on. A figure not unlike a black superhero in red tights with the word CUBA across his chest came running down the boulevard, looked me in the eyes and rushed past me at a good clip. People applauded as he went by them and he'd now and then fist pump the air in acknowledgment.

"Who is that guy?" I asked a pedestrian.

"He's a former 400-meter Olympic sprinter," answered the middle-aged man, "I forget his name, but he runs here once in a while in his old national uniform to show off and get a hand. Everybody knows him and what he's up to and they lead him on." I thanked him and went on, smiling at this part of the Cuban character that is so accommodating of idiosyncrasy.

After a few more blocks, I encountered one of the grandest scenes of my stroll: El Paseo del Prado, a relic and testament to one of Spain's great traditions, the promenade. This was Havana's first paved street, dating back to the late 18th century. Marble benches lined the walk, shaded by twin rows of trees that faded in green plumes into the distance where about a kilometer away loomed the dome of the capitol. In the fading light, elaborate cast iron lampposts already mustered their lights along the walk. I took some photos then decided to sit for a bit to rest on one of the benches at the entrance to the promenade. A red-haired man in his thirties came and sat next to me and said hello. When he found out I had been born in Havana and was back after 50 years, he asked me if the changes I'd seen had pleased me. My first impulse was caution, for I didn't know if he'd been following me or if his question was just a ruse to get information concerning what *they* care the most about: ideology. He noticed my hesitation and said, "Don't worry, even if I were from the government, what are they going to do with an American citizen?"

"How about arrest him on trumped-up charges of espionage?"

"Well, if you don't want to answer, nobody's going to force you."

"Why do you want to know my opinion?"

"I'm always interested to hear what foreigners think of Cuba, and you especially since you were here before and have just come back. It's a pretty natural question, isn't it?"

"I noticed you weren't at all shocked when I said, 'How about arrest him on trumped-up charges of espionage?' You expect such things from your government?"

"No, but I expect a Miami Cuban to believe such things about our government. So it didn't surprise me you said it."

"But you also didn't exactly jump at the chance to defend the honesty and integrity of your government."

"OK, to be honest, I know such things might happen here and we both know the government rules, shall we say, strictly."

"OK, I'll be honest with you; I've seen some good things here and some bad things. But I've seen more bad things than good things."

El Capitolio from El Paseo del Prado. Cuba's first paved street and a monument of the Spanish tradition of the promenade.

"Really? Like what?"

"The people don't eat well."

"Do you see anyone starving, or looking for food in the garbage?"

"No, but they eat a dull and monotonous diet, their choices are limited, and they get by in spite of the system."

"But everyone eats and nobody starves, isn't that the most important thing?"

"Is it necessary to have a communist state in order to make sure everyone eats?"

"So eating well is more important than ... ideology?"

"I think the most important things in the world are the things that happen to you every day and eating badly or eating just to subsist, this happens to you every day. And to answer your question yes, eating well is more important than ideology and, in this case, if the ideology you believe in results in subsistence nourishment, that's never a good sign."

"I like what you just said."

"What?"

"That the most important things in life are the things that happen to you every day. It's so simple but so true."

"Listen I have to go, it's getting late. Nice talking to you." We shook hands and I walked off toward the Malecón. I looked back after a dozen steps, but he was gone.

Then I came across another lesser promenade, the one leading to the Palacio Presidencial, last occupied by the previous dictator, Fulgencio Batista, now being remodeled into a museum. Here a multitude of boys was playing soccer using the space between the legs of parallel opposite benches along the promenade as goals. "Now this is new," I thought, for Cubans have been traditionally a two-sport people, baseball and boxing, with basketball a distant third. Now there was this new zeal for soccer, a sport absent from the island when I left. One of the boys saw me taking pictures, looked at me then at the camera and came to the conclusion that I was rich. He pinched his thin belly and with the other hand employed a universal gesture of eating—he joined his fingers at their tips and thrust them a few times at his mouth, in his eyes, a plea for mercy. I could feel my eyes softening, so I dug out a few coins. He yanked them out of my hand and walked away without a mere thank you. Another boy saw him counting and came running

El Palacio Presidencial. A *bicitaxi* much like the one Eli took me everywhere in is in the foreground. The soccer playing, belly-pinching boys are beyond, still innocent of our soon-to-be encounter.

at me holding out his hand and with the other trying to pinch his stomach, feigning that he could find no flesh to hold. I dug for a few more coins and put them in his hand. He took them and yelled to the other boys, "Hey!" and pointed with his head at me. Suddenly, a crowd of boys surrounded me, tugging at my shirt, patting their stomachs and hopping around me. I tried to walk away saying "*No más, no más!*" But they would not relent their yelling and jerking; finally I took out all the coins and threw them up in the air behind me and the boys fell upon them like lions at a kill. I hastened away to the Parque Central and got into a beautiful 1956 Chevrolet Bel Air. On the way back to El Vedado, the driver, like so many during my trip, confessed his disappointment with the revolution.

Back in my room, exhausted after the long walk, I showered and got in bed thinking back on the extraordinary afternoon. That in such a short time and space I had encountered so much that was telling and thought-provoking struck me as remarkable. Cuba's uniqueness, its contrast to the rest of the world, engenders in anyone able to see its implications a torrent of ideas. If people come here just to experience the white sand beaches, the music, and the mojitos, they will miss the great abstract world the island would sire in their mind. I took out my journal and, shoving aside the exhaustion, wrote for over an hour to make sure nothing was forgotten. My last thought was "It's a writer's paradise. No wonder Hemingway loved this island." I faded to black.

Day Seven

Silvio was cooking breakfast as I sat at the table and sipped on a *café con leche*. The room beyond the living room served as a combination kitchen, dining room, and study. Photos of a famous ballet dancer and other well-known artists from Latin America hung on one wall. Sandra was at the study conversing with me as she answered e-mails at an old PC. "We're very lucky you know. Not everyone in Cuba has an e-mail account," she was saying.

"How were you able to get one?" I asked.

"It's a privilege for many years of service and of course I convinced the Ministry of Communications that it was indispensable for our little retirement business."

She had told me that she had been a performance coordinator for artistic events and that Silvio had been a tourism industry alimentary specialist (in other words, a chef). They were now retired, living on their pensions (hers was $15 and his was $10 a month) and they made ends meet by renting the room next door to tourists that would write to a state-run Website that would in turn provide them with the e-mail addresses of those that showed interest in staying in their room.

"Why is it so difficult to get an e-mail account?" I asked, adding, "Anyone can get an account free in Costa Rica or anywhere else I know of."

"It's the Yankees," said Silvio as he turned over an omelet. "They restricted the cables that feed the Internet to Cuba. So we have limited access that can only be given to a select few." Silvio was, of course, feeding me the party line on the Internet. Although initially the U.S. embargo delayed an undersea cable and made computers, routers and other equipment expensive and difficult to obtain, in 2009 President Obama announced that the U.S. would allow its companies to provide Internet service to Cuba. The Cuban government rejected the offer and started working with the Chávez regime in Venezuela.

"But do you actually have access to the Internet or do you just have an e-mail account?" I continued.

"Oh, no, I just have e-mail, which costs 1.50 CUC per hour," replied Sandra, "The Internet would be too expensive, about 4.50 CUC per hour.

"Do you get many guests?" I asked Sandra.

"We used to, but since the recession it has been really slow." I asked her if the government imposed taxes on their business.

"Oh, yes, we have to pay a fixed amount, about 50 CUC, every month regardless of sales."

"So you mean that you still have to pay if you get no one?"

"Yes, and some months we have to sell something or borrow just to cope."

"You know in most countries taxes are based on percentages, not fixed charges..."

"Here's your breakfast. *Buen provecho!*"

I ate the full breakfast while they drank coffee with a pastry. As I ate I could sense Sandra observing me while Silvio and I talked small. "Forgive me for prying," said Sandra, "but since you're traveling alone, I was wondering if you were married or not."

"Do I look like I should be married?"

"Frankly, yes. You do. You seem to be a very refined person. I should think you'd make someone very happy. Isn't that right, Silvio?"

"Absolutely, he's refined and personable. He'd make a great husband!"

I could feel myself blushing and all I could say was, "That's very kind of you. But no I'm not married, never have been." I looked at them and I could see that this was not enough of an explanation, so I went on. "I guess I've always put marriage on the backburner in favor of traveling and seeing the world, and I don't mean as a tourist, but living and working where I went. I've lived and worked in 7 countries and visited about 25 others. Also, I've been a little unlucky with love. When she loved me, I didn't, and when I loved her, she didn't. Just one of those things."

"That's the way of love most of the time," answered Sandra. That's why Silvio and I... It's been special for 51 years now."

"Congratulations, that is special. Most of my friends have experienced divorce, including my own brother, who's been married three times now, like he's a Hollywood movie star! Anyway, I feel you're very good people as well. Besides I think only good people can stay married that long."

"But you know," said Silvio, "the government, I mean this society that the revolution has built helps people stay together."

"Really? How's that, Silvio?"

"Well, maybe in capitalist societies the constant need and worry about making money and all the importance they attach to it causes a lot of disunion in couples. You know, here we never have to worry about money; one way or another the government always provides a way. And health care is guaranteed for all. They have built one of the best health care systems in the world right here in this little island. Why look at Chávez he came here to be treated for his cancer and they cured him!"

"Well, you seem to have everything you need and you appear to be in good health, so what more does anyone need, besides each other? But even this you have achieved. So you know, Silvio, you may be right about that the struggle for money may cause conflict. Some of the happiest people in the world have little money and it's almost proverbial that rich people are often very unhappy. Besides, the more possessions you have the more you have to worry about, the more complex your life becomes and the more distraction from what are the really important things, which as the proverb says, the best are free. There's a lot to be said for minimalism, or simplicity in life. Why just yesterday I took a walk along the Malecón and I saw something wonderful..." Of course, I went on to tell them about that street scene and they were grateful that I had seen the value of the Revolution.

We talked a little more on this topic and then Sandra asked, "What about your birth certificate, did you get it certified?" I explained about my visit to the lawyer's and that today I planned to go again to check the progress. Sandra said, "Don't worry about this; we can take care of picking it up and sending it to you in Costa Rica."

"Oh Sandra, that's too much to ask."

"You didn't ask, I offered. No, I think I can speak for both when I tell you how much we value our new friend. Isn't that right, Silvio?"

"Absolutely, it would be a pleasure for us. Besides, we don't get out much and it would be a good excuse to get some exercise."

"Silvio!" retorted Sandra, "How can you be so utilitarian? Don't listen to him, Gabriel; we do this from the bottom of our hearts."

"I didn't take it like that, Sandra. Besides, we men are by nature utilitarian. Right Silvio?" Silvio nodded smiling, relieved.

Back in my room I updated my journal about this conversation. I was glad I had again resisted the impulse to contradict my new friends and get into a useless dispute. Although their blind support for what is by any sane conclusion a repressive totalitarian state was incongruous with their educational level, especially Sandra's, they were plainly so kind and sweet-natured that they disarmed me. Now, my motive for self-control was not only my deference to their advanced age but also that I liked them. That well-educated people could maintain such a stance was not unprecedented, for the wrong kind of education, a politicized education, can be used to make a people subservient. The Germans, one of the best-educated people in the world, fell just short of voting a psychopath into power and eventually either at worst embraced him or at best decided to look the other way. And when I was teaching at the University of Santiago de Compostela in Galicia, Spain, in the mid–1980s, my students, by and large leftists, were somehow convinced that the Berlin Wall had been erected not to keep the East Germans in, but to keep the West Germans out! I turned to the pictures on the dresser. If one just replaced the July 26th Movement armband with a swastika one, Silvio's photo under the glass could have been of a Hitler Youth. The same superiority, the same arrogance of the eyes dared the viewer to disagreement. So what had that Castro Youth fathered? An agreeable old man who injected the party line propaganda into almost any utterance. I wondered what he might turn into if contradicted. What shook me was the thought that the power of control of information and education over a people is incalculable. How can people be so plastic? So Skinnerian?

In Costa Rica, suborning a government official for anything from a traffic ticket to a building permit is almost expected. On the way to the lawyer's office in a comical 1955 Ford Fairlane, I considered bribing the lawyer, Mrs. Hurtado, to hurry the certification process. But the thought faded as I considered how much it would confirm in her eyes the stereotypical view of Americans—that we thought money was everything and could accomplish anything. I hated the idea of proving her right.

"I'm sorry Gabriel," she said, "but yesterday I went to the Costa Rican embassy on your behalf, but I'm afraid that the certification was not done yet. They told me tomorrow it should be ready to be sent to the Ministry of External Affairs. But I'll be honest with you, it will take at least five working days for the ministry to certify it."

"I can't thank you enough for going out of your way for me, Mrs. Hurtado. But look, I have some friends willing to act on my behalf after I leave. Can they pick up the certificate for me? I don't have to sign anything ahead of time?"

"No. There's nothing to sign; if you give me their names now, I can release the certificate to them when they come."

"Wonderful. You've been very professional. Thank you." She nodded with her eyes the most beautiful nod of the eyes I had yet seen in Cuba. We arranged for Sandra and Silvio to pick up the document and I left.

In the taxi back to Casa Sandra, I felt a strange relief. I had done all I could and the solution was down to my new friends. How bizarre life can be, I reflected. Here I was back in Cuba after 50 years and I had wound up depending on a nice couple whose only quality that normally would have impeded our friendship was their ideology. I had bridged the Great Divide by simply keeping my mouth shut. All I had to do was to continue doing so and I would have my birth certificate. This last thought shamed me. For a moment, I felt as if I were using them. Then I remembered that I *liked* them. I considered that if the Cuban Revolution had never happened, I would have easily become their friend. The blur of buildings down the canyon of Calle Linea streamed by, my mind floated back to when the Great Divide began...

The sunlight is orange. There. A good stone. I pick it up to throw it at the light post on the corner. My arm stops. *"Viva la Revolución!"*

"Viva!"

"Viva Fidel!"

"Viva!" Soldiers. Many, many soldiers in green. All with beards, with rifles. Carry red and black flags. March up the hill shouting, push

their rifles at the sky. Rosaries around their necks. Green caps. Black berets. Smell grass, sweat, urine. All smiling but mad. I turn around. Mother's arms.

"Mami, why are those soldiers going up the hill to our school?"

"I don't know, my son. I don't know."

"Are they good soldiers, Mami?"

"Yes, my son, they're good soldiers. Let's go inside."

That was the last day my brother and I went to school in Cuba. In its infancy, we sacrificed and gave all to the Revolution. Everyone did so since it was all about a dream come true. The whole island was enchanted with their liberators, the bearded guerrillas that had come down from the mountains of Oriente and swept westward, winning battle after battle, town after town. The day they freed Holguín, a large city in Oriente where my family lived, they marched by our house up the hill that led to our school at the top and turned it into a temporary headquarters. When the rebels arrived at my father's farm 24 kilometers from Holguín, he gladly slaughtered some cattle for them to eat and housed them until they marched on towards the west.

Later, after the fall of Havana and the flight of the dictator to Spain, there were street celebrations for a fairytale month. A wide-eyed glimmer of innocence shone in all eyes cast on the parading heroes. Fidel spoke in Havana's Cuartel Colombia, later christened Ciudad Libertad, in front of tens of thousands. In mid-speech, a white dove fluttered to his shoulder and two others perched on the podium, vanquishing the last doubt that he was the God-sent savior. People connected with Christ his beard and that he and 12 men had survived the initial skirmish with Batista's troops. An aura of perfection imbued everything about *los barbudos*, "the bearded ones." A camaraderie, goodwill and informality unheard of in the island's history overcame the people and indeed, they began to greet each other with *camarada* or comrade, as was the custom among the conquering rebels. They would turn Cuba into a true democracy; the people, *los camaradas*, after a long spell under the dictator's thumb, were now in charge.

Then signs that things were not what they seemed emerged. The words "collectivism" and "socialism" were often heard from leaders. There was the execution of Colonel Cornelio Rojas, whose head was blown off by a firing squad on national television. He had been the respected Santa Clara chief of police, whose summary execution was ordered by Che Guevara. The lynch mob methods used in the public trials judging officers and policemen under Batista shocked my father's sensibilities as a lawyer—hearsay was accepted as evidence. The Morro Castle, the ancient colonial fortress that guarded the entrance to Havana Harbor became a dungeon, where hundreds were shot without trial. And the use of the greeting "comrade" was tied to the Soviet custom. Then came the first night they harrassed us.

My brother and I were watching TV in the living room. Mother was sewing, father, reading.

Ta ta ta ta…. Ta ta ta ta…

"Who's there?" My father asked the door.

"Is this the home of Don Facundo?

"Yes."

"We are the Revolutionary Army. Open the door." Papa opened the door. Six men stood in the dark. They barged in past my father and filled the room with their smell of leather and gun oil, their olive green, machine guns, and boots.

"We're here to search the house."

"What for?"

"We're looking for counterrevolutionary evidence and weapons. You two upstairs. You two in the back." The four men disappeared.

"Look, you have a court order to do this?"

"Not needed. We're defending the Revolution. This is how we're doing things for now. Where's your identification? I'll need your wife's too." Father reached for his wallet, took out his license and handed it to the soldier. Mother looked for her purse, opened it with nervous fingers and found her card and handed it to the other man. Upstairs, the sounds of drawers opening, furniture dragging, clothes hangers screeching, papers rustling, books slapping closed. In the back, the clanging of pots and the grating of cutlery and tools, the banging of cabinet doors. Then the bootsteps coming down the stairs. The two men were holding father's Winchesters.

"Look what we found, lieutenant." He passed the lieutenant one of the rifles. He eyed the mother of pearl inlaid stock and the carved scrollwork, weighed it, checked the lever action.

"We have to confiscate these."

125

"Gentlemen, those are obviously collector's special editions and antiques. They're both over 80 years old," protested my father.

"They can still shoot?"

"Well, of course, I keep them in condition."

"Then they can be used against the Revolution. Anything else boys?"

"*Nada*," said one of the men who had been in the back.

"Come now, gentlemen. Look at me. Do I look threatening to you? As you can see, I'm no spring chicken. Don't tell me you actually envision me with a cowboy hat firing off rounds against the Revolution with these Winchesters like John Wayne!" He managed to get a chuckle out of a few of the men.

"Sorry, Don Facundo. We have our orders.

"Very well take the rifles, then. But aren't you even going to tell me what made you come here in the first place?"

"We have reliable sources that have indicated you may not be happy with the Revolution, Don Facundo. I advise you to be careful."

Of course, he was lying. The reason was that people who had been well off were suspected counter-revolutionaries just because they had something to lose with the Revolution. But as time went by, my father would not keep his mouth shut. He was a lawyer and it was his nature to opine. Once I overheard mother chastise him for openly criticizing the Revolution. The next time they came they took him away for interrogation. But the old man was a charmer and trained persuader, so he always returned.

Back at Casa Sandra I explained to Sandra and Silvio what had happened at the lawyer's. They assured me that they would pick up the certificate and send it to me. I invited them to dinner that evening at the private restaurant Silvio had mentioned the first day, La Pachanga. Their eyes lit up and we decided on eight o'clock.

That evening we strolled to the restaurant through the orange light and blue shadows. After four blocks, we came upon one of the few neon signs I saw in Havana, La Pachanga. Entering, the smell of good food enveloped us. A narrow two-story building, the first floor was set up not unlike an American fast food joint, with the back-lit photographs of dishes on the wall behind a counter where clients could

My father, the finest orator I've ever known, speaking in praise of the newly crowned Miss Holguín in Holguín, Cuba, circa 1956. The speech was being radio broadcast. His charm, charisma and persuasive skills likely kept him from extended residence in Castro's prisons.

order without waiter service and sit in small round tables on either side of the passage in front of the entrance. Silvio said the real restaurant was on the second floor, so we climbed the stairs which opened into a windowless room painted in black and lit with neon signs, fish tanks, and spotlights. Soft techno music backdropped the clientele's chatter. We sat at the only available table and soon a waiter arrived with a menu. I ordered a bottle of wine and three glasses. I knew what I wanted, my longed-for Cuban Sandwich. Sandra and Silvio settled on the roast chicken. The prices were a little less than those of a decent diner in the U.S.—the sandwich was five CUC's; the roast chicken, six—although I wondered how an average Cuban could afford them.

127

"These prices are high for Cubans, aren't they?

"Yes," said Sandra. "I'm sure most of these clients work in the tourism industry and they get tips from foreigners. Some may be taxi drivers, some waiters. That's how they can afford it. We normally don't come here unless we've had a good month." The waiter came again and we ordered. The result did not disappoint—the real McCoy.

"Mama mia!" I chirped, "Now that is a Cuban Sandwich!"

"I told you, didn't I," said Silvio inevitably. "Of course, Raúl was right in letting these small businesses develop. People always care more if the business is their own and it reflects in the products. A state restaurant can never match this quality."

"I agree, Silvio. It's like taking care of your own car versus a rental." Little did Silvio know what I was really thinking: "Why in heaven can't you extend what you just said to everything in a society and understand how much better the quality of life would be? What must they have taught you for you to blot out reason and blind you to what is so obvious? Why aren't you resentful it took so long?"

The rest of our dinner was pleasant and uneventful, except when I told my guests that it surprised me that in Cuba, having such a grand musical tradition, a restaurant owner would choose European techno as the background music. Sandra sent for the waiter and then asked me, "What would you like to hear?"

"Please put on Israel López 'Cachao,' if you have it."

"Of course we have Cachao, the inventor of the mambo," said the waiter, adding, "It's gratifying that a foreigner knows our music so well, thank you, sir."

Within minutes, the sassy lamentations of Cachao's Master Sessions floated in the air and the guests and staff were visibly grateful for the change.

"Sometimes we forget who we are because of familiarity," said Silvio. "It's good that you reminded us."

"You know what? The same thing happens in every culture I've ever known well enough. The old adage is 'familiarity breeds contempt,' right?"

"So true. And our young people have recently turned to foreign influences like rap or reggaeton and ignored our great tradition," said Silvio. "Fortunately, our government still supports the classics as well as all musicians who pursue them."

"That's right, Silvio." Then I explained to them how impressed I had been with the performance I had attended at the Jazz Café and my conversation with the bartender. My strategy was still to steer clear of political discord with my new friends. What was remarkable about the remainder of our conversation that evening was not so much what was said, but what was not. It struck me that here again they were in the presence of their new Cuban-American friend and they did not take the opportunity to ask me anything about life in America or anywhere else I had been. It was as if they had nothing to learn about the world, as if they already knew all there was to know about the outside, although the only trip abroad either of them had taken was Sandra's long ago trip to the Soviet Union. Were they afraid to learn? Afraid of finding a contradiction to what they knew or thought they knew about the world? Or was it simply a kind of hubris from years of indoctrination that had assured them of the corruption and savagery of the outside and convinced them of the superiority, nurture and protection of the nest?

As we walked home, I started to experience a dry hacking cough. The remaining days I mostly dedicated to taking advantage of Havana's nightlife. I had little choice as a heatwave descended on the city and made walking outside intolerable from nine to four. I suspected the cough was from the heavy Venezuelan leaded gas burned by those American classics, Russian Ladas or East German Trabants. So I stayed in my room reading Dostoevsky, writing in the journal and flicking through the few available channels from time to time. I had heard that CNN had an office in Cuba and was expecting to see CNN International. But it never happened. After my return to Costa Rica, I learned that CNN used to be on the air in Cuba, but that the regime had shut it down in 2009. I watched a few movies, all Hollywood flicks. Maybe it was my sensitivity or maybe it was because Hollywood is unabashed in its portrayal of American society, but I got the impression that the only American movies the government played were those that painted the U.S. as a corrupt, violent and drug-addled society.

Day Eight

The cough had subsided enough that in mid-afternoon I went back to Old Havana for more photos. I went to the old Chinatown, *El Barrio Chino*, behind the Capitolio. It struck me that, like every Chinatown I had visited in the world, it seemed prosperous. Little wonder that China, whose people had been unleashed since Deng Xiaoping had pronounced that "to be rich is glorious," had become such an economic juggernaut. I marveled at the power of the dark forces that had kept a culturally enterprising and hard-working people manacled in poverty for fifty years, only to discover belatedly the madness of Mao.

Leaving Chinatown and heading for El Malecón, I came across one of the government *bodegas* that supply every neighborhood with subsidized goods. The shelves were empty save for the odd bag of powdered milk or sugar. Standing outside, I took a shot of the empty shelves that included a sign that uselessly listed the price of a host of items. An old blotched woman emerged empty-handed, looked at me as I took a photo and said, "You Yankees! You have no right to come here and take pictures!"

"I'm no Yankee, lady, and you don't even know that taking pictures is a human right." She snorted at me and limped away mumbling to herself. I also went off mumbling to myself, looking at the blue Caribbean horizon at the end of the street beyond EL Malecón. Mumbling at the insanity, the absurdity of what the Castros had done. Like the Chinese, the Cuban people are by nature enterprising and talented. The most successful minority community in the history of the United States lay 90 miles beyond that horizon, an example of what Latins can achieve in an accountable society. "If only these bastards would let them go." Dejected, I walked to EL Malecón, took some shots of the Castle and decided to go back to the Capitolio to take a taxi to Casa Sandra. On the way, I went by some ministry whose members were spilling out. All were dressed in leather street shoes, good slacks, and fine linen *guayaberas*, in effect, better than all but a few Cubans. Many got in new Japanese or German cars parked nearby. "I see. Uh-huh. Nothing new here," again, mumbling to myself.

A block later I stopped to observe a man sitting on a stool in the sidewalk. He had a short line of people standing and waiting for his service. Coming closer, I realized he was refilling BIC lighters with fluid. A sign next to him read: *Recarga de Encendedores* (Lighter Refill). So as not to interrupt the man, I asked a man who had just had his lighter refilled, "Excuse me, sir, how much does he charge for a refill?"

"Sure, it's 5 cents."

"Is this a licensed job he has or is he just freelancing?" I asked in a low discreet voice.

He looked around and said, "Here, let's move over here and I'll explain." He took me by the elbow and we crossed the street. Then he said, "I didn't want to say this there because I'm not sure if he is licensed or not. So to answer your question, yes, he's supposed to have a license, but maybe he has one, maybe not. I can't tell and I don't want to know anyway. Why did you want to know?"

Lighter refilling in Old Havana, a state licensed job that includes repair service. No one throws away their BIC's in Cuba.

"I was just curious. You see, in Costa Rica, where I live, nobody ever refills lighters; they just throw them away and buy a new one."

"Really? That's very wasteful, isn't it? Why don't people refill their lighters?

"I guess it's because they find it more convenient to just throw them away and get a new one."

"What's the monthly salary in Costa Rica?"

"About $500 a month."

"That's why. A lighter here costs about 1 CUC, so no wonder."

I thanked him and he walked off lighting a cigarette with his new refill. I walked on a little farther and came upon another sidewalk service. This was a *zapatero*, a shoe repair service. Countless shoes surrounded the man, who was hammering one over an anvil that was shaped like the sole of a shoe. The "anvil" looked like the footrests that shoeshines use in the States at airports. Judging from the number of shoes business seemed brisk and as I watched a client came by and asked for his pair by presenting a ticket. The repairman matched it with a ticket attached to one of the pairs and exchanged the shoes for what seemed a few pennies.

They don't make BIC lighters or shoes or carbonated sodas any cheaper just for the Cuban market, so Cubans have to buy these imports at world prices that are onerous for their poor salaries. The regime helps by providing every citizen with a free pair of shoes every year. As we all know from personal experience, this is not enough, so the shoe repair industry as well as the lighter refill service are "big business" in Cuba. If Cubans buy something in a plastic container they tend to keep the container after it's empty, for it can be used for everything from a potable water refill to a plant pot to a toilet tank float. Because of this, in contrast to our absurd "throw away society," nothing goes to waste in Cuba. Many retirees supplement their 10 CUC per month pensions by recycling aluminum and plastic. On more than one occasion, I saw older men carrying huge amounts of recyclables tied into enormous bundles on their backs to take them to recycling centers. I also witnessed how people go shopping by always taking their own bag or container to carry back whatever they buy.

Seeing all this called to mind how wasteful we are in the West. I asked myself how many of us employ the little extra time and effort to take along a bag when we go shopping. How many of our businesses dispense goods in bulk, expecting their clients to bring their own containers? Not many in either case. I suppose our time is too valuable for such trifles. But who has ingrained in us that our time is so pricey that we can't be bothered with small matters that can help save the planet from choking in its own garbage? Probably the same people who put the saying "Time is money" on the pedestal of our consciousness.

I took a side street farther on and walked along it for a while. Passing by several buildings, as always in Old Havana, stuck together without any space dividing them, I could see the squalor that many Cubans live in. Yes, the government provides free housing, but it's not the kind that you can ask the landlord to come and fix anything that goes wrong in the building. Cubans have to do it themselves. This is the deal. But since most people have neither the money nor the resources to do it, most buildings continue in disrepair until the inevitable *derrumbe*, that is, collapse. Going by one building that was on concrete stilts, apparently to provide parking under the structure in days gone by, a thousand

A dilapidated house; a sight too common in Old Havana.

133

leaks oozed from the walls and ceiling, leaving a large seething puddle on the floor. What made the puddle seethe I didn't care to find out, but it stank of death and putrescence. I wondered at the origins of the leaks. How many damaged toilets, drains, water pipes, bathtubs and sinks combined to cause the building to appear to bleed from a collective jugular? What kind of lives were lived in it? Lives accustomed to heat, humidity, fungi and grime. How long before the implacable liquid eroded the concrete and corroded the steel that braced the whole? Again, I didn't care to find out, but the residents would someday and it might be their last perception of the world.

I walked to the Parque Central and took a taxi back to Casa Sandra. This time I didn't bother to ask the driver of the blue and yellow 1957 Buick about the Revolution. He asked me, "What do you think of the Revolution?" I looked at him with what must have seemed to him the wary eye. So he added, "Don't worry; we're alone and besides, you're a foreigner." This time it was my turn to confess my feelings about the Revolution. The driver absolved me.

At 10 p.m., I was in front of another famous nightclub, La Zorra y el Cuervo (The Fox and the Crow). I took the stairs down to a basement and walked in along a long bar that led to a room of tables in front of the stage. I sat at the bar's corner, ordered a mojito and a Monte Cristo No 5. The room was filling up for the start of the band at 11. Soon a tourist sat next to me. He was in his late 40's and from the old East Berlin. "Were you at the Wall when it came down?" I asked, figuring he'd be in his early twenties at that time.

"Of course. Everyone in Berlin was at that stupid wall that day. Even saw David Hasselhoff, remember him? He sing that song *Looking for Freedom*. He had a leather jacket with, how you say lights that come on and off?"

"Blinking?"

"Yes, blinking lights. That song was very popular underground in the East that time and there he appeared with his blinking lights jacket. It was magic."

"Was the support for change 100 percent?" I asked.

"I cannot say 100 percent because there is always some crazies. You know, strong head communists. But I say 99 percent. But you know we were so happy, so full of hope, because you know in the East you go to work in a good for nothing work then you go home and you just have your schnapps or vodka in a private life with friends you trust and that was your only freedom. Your public life was dull and gray and always careful and pretending. We all hated that stupid life. Sick of it. But you know even with all being so happy, so full of hope, one part of us was afraid. Because we know nothing about the future and what the changes bring." I told him about my experience as a professor in Spain and what my students thought the Wall was for. "I know those people," he continued. "Without those guys we win our freedom years before. Stupid people in the West Europe who know nothing, just, how you say? Theoretic?

"Theory."

"Yes, theory. Nothing real. This is why we are always thanking the Americans. They were the only country supported us."

The band came on and we broke off the political conversation and turned to intermittent comments about music. A great band it was until the end at one in the morning. We exchanged e-mail addresses telling each other that if we ever found ourselves in our respective countries *mi casa es tu casa*. We said goodbye and good luck and I took a taxi home.

Writing everything down in bed in my room, I pondered the improbable kinship the East German, Klaus, and I shared. Our families had borne the yoke of the same tyranny, although we had been 5,000 miles apart—the same, if not worse for him and his, for after the fall of the Wall the victims of the Stasi dug up the measure of its brutality.

Thursday, November 9, 1989. I remember that day as clearly as the day Kennedy was shot. I was alone in my six *tatami* bedroom in Osaka. The steel of the morning sun blanched the screen that bore the images of a night 10,000 miles away. As I beheld the child-like joy in those faces now filled with the essence of the human spirit, a great weight rose from my chest and knotted itself around my throat and finally dripped from my face in the shape of tears. If someone had been watching, she would have witnessed the lurch and heave of my shoulders, heard the sighs and sobs as I craned to take in, to share the glory of the moment with those who had known and lived true oppression.

And I'm not talking about the virtually imagined oppression that

Sting felt when he wrote the lyrics to the antiwar song *Russians* or Pink Floyd's exaggerated lamentations of modern British life in *The Wall*. I was in Spain teaching at the University of Santiago de Compostela when these two musical pieces came out and I can assure the reader in no uncertain terms that the left, surely impulsed by Soviet propaganda, viewed and painted them as evidence of the evil of the West. Consequently, in the 1980's a leftist backlash surged against the efforts of two leaders who ultimately would be on the right side of history in their struggle against real oppression: Ronald Reagan and Margaret Thatcher.

While I understand the spirit and sentiment behind Sting's antiwar cry, which to his credit at least denounced both sides in the madness of the nuclear race, it was a form of fence sitting in the middle of a struggle between good and evil. By treating both sides equally, Sting lent legitimacy to the evil side. While during what is referred to as the Last Good War, an antiwar song might have been intellectually acceptable, pragmatically, however, it would have been risible, for in those days it was clear what had to be done and peace was not the way to do it. The same goes for what I consider the real last good war, the Cold War. It's important to understand who and what we in the West were dealing with: The collective death toll perpetrated by just the USSR and China in the 20th century was by conservative estimates 65 million of their own people; by liberal estimates, over 100 million people were systematically eliminated (this last figure doubles the total death toll of Word War II). The song *Russians*' most memorable quatrain, the one the youth of Europe latched on to, referred to Reagan's claiming that he would protect us from the Russians, Sting's rejection of this approach, followed by the refrain we are all very familiar with about the Russians also loving their children. Poetic license aside, the Russians had nothing to do with it. Rather, it was a despicable mafia in power called the Soviet Communist Party that in no way represented the Russian people. And the fact remains that Mr. Reagan was really trying to protect us *and* the Russian people, albeit in the perverse logic of the nuclear arms race.

While Pink Floyd pitched the evils of British society in *The Wall*, employing in the movie version images of the nightmare of *1984* to represent the British educational system, the real wall and the real *1984* were 600 miles away in Berlin and beyond. It should be noted that Roger Waters' suffering under his mother's tutelage and the "horrible" British system pales in comparison to real suffering. In the end, Mr. Waters was educated well enough to write fine lyrics and earn millions through a system that allowed him all the freedom of expression in his heart's desire while behind the real wall people lived entire lives with muzzles across their mouths for fear of death or imprisonment in the Gulag. Meanwhile, the Soviets used Pink Floyd, Sting and others of similar leanings as propaganda tools so well that my students thought the Berlin Wall was erected in order to keep the West out. In those days, very popular was the preposterous idea that Ronald Reagan represented the real Big Brother of *1984*. In other words the only Western leader to challenge Gorbachev to "tear down this wall" was the evil one. The widespread acceptance of the lyrics of *The Wall* and *Russians* as indicative of the evil of the West showed the extent to which so many had bought into the Soviet propaganda, hence Lenin's famous phrase "our useful idiots in the West."

Such ironies led the former president of the Ivory Coast, Félix Houphouët-Boigny, to once declare, "Send your son to Moscow and he will return an anti-communist; send him to the Sorbonne and he will return a communist." In the end, the system Sting and Pink Floyd condemned empowered them to do much for themselves, but they in turn did little for Klaus and the millions behind the Iron Curtain. Instead, they went with the trend and current of the time. Meanwhile, 136 East Germans died trying to flee the Berlin of the "German Democratic Republic."

Back in my room in 1989 Osaka, my heart flew from me with the hope of what the fall of the Berlin Wall might mean for Cuba. But as the 1990s would play themselves out, Castro adapted and the Revolution survived.

Day Nine

To avoid the daytime heat and also because I was running low in cash (my debit cards were useless in Cuba since they were from American banks), I saved my last day for an evening in Old Havana. I went out at around seven, taking a taxi *colectivo* to the Capitol. A band was playing that I could hear from the plaza, so I followed the music straight to the Montserrate, where I ordered a mojito and sat at the bar listening to old standards.

As usual in the smaller venues in Havana, there were no mikes and the band played as honestly as a band can play so that the singer had to be a real singer with a voice that projected and filled the space before it, so the dynamics had to be effected by the varying pressure of the fingers and hands or the force of the diaphragm against the instrument and the coordination of the musicians. When one visits Cuba one of the finest things to behold is a band in the raw like bands used to be for the greater part of history, before electronics began to dismantle one of music's most treasured components, its heart and humanity. One must admire how the Revolution has supported the arts and, in particular, its music and its musicians, surely Cuba's greatest gifts to humanity.

I drank the mojito and listened, a part of me hoping that Gretel, the engineer turned prostitute, would walk through the door and at least keep me company. Pondering how to go about that evening, I decided to go bar-hopping along Calle Obispo; it was Friday evening and bands would be playing in many places, including EL Floridita, Hemingway's old haunt where he drank his daiquirís. But first I had to find it. I was surprised when the bartender told me it was on the next corner on the right, where Calle Obispo begins its journey to the Plaza Vieja.

The gold of the evening sun warmed me as I walked to the next corner. But there was wetness in the air and thunder in the distance.

Beggars waited at the corner entrance. They had seen me coming, seen how I was dressed and already had their hands out before I arrived. I emptied my pocket of coins and went inside. The sun streamed in through the row of tall windows facing the street. By the entrance a woman, who had seen better days but still had a few good left, sang a bolero accompanied by a guitarist, a conga player, and the din of the guests. A long bar on the left ran half the length of the club. White tablecloths streamed over the tables between the bar and the windows draped with red curtains. Waiters in white vests and bow ties scurried among the guests carrying steaming seafood plates and Martini glasses brimming with the lemon yellow of the daiquirí. El Floridita was a posh old bar by any standard. I ambled to a stool at mid-bar, ordered a daiquirí and then, around the elbow of the bar, smiling right at me I

"He was stiff all right, not from the daiquirís he famously imbibed, but from the bronze that made him." Ernest Hemingway's statue at El Floridita. The open book on the bar is *The Old Man and the Sea*, also in bronze. The photo of Castro listening to him is in the background.

saw Ernest Hemingway. He was stiff all right, not from the daiquirís he famously imbibed, but from the bronze that made him. I held up the daiquirí toward him and drank a good long draft. Instantly refreshing. Turning toward the trio as it played *Guantanamera*, then back at Hemingway, now being photographed with a couple who had their arms around him, I realized I was in a classic tourist haven. The bar's Cuban population was in waiter's garb; the rest were tourists, that lower life form that is condemned by its nature to the ridiculous. The thought that I was one of them didn't evade me and I took refuge in that at least I wore no shorts and had no camera.

Encouraged by the first one, I ordered another daiquirí and a Romeo y Julieta as a well-dressed man in his forties took the stool next to me. The bartender returned carrying a tray with the daiquirí, the cigar in an ashtray, a long match and a cigar cutter all arranged in the

The Cuban cigar is only becoming in women when they reach a certain age. It happens when the woman is done with the last vestige of her vanity and she can at long last enjoy the consolation of a good cigar.

center. Laying the items on the bar in the same order as on the tray, he asked me if I wanted him to cut the cigar and I consented. He snipped just enough of the tip to open a passage for air, leaving a rounded lip on the tip so it would not disintegrate as I smoked. Then he handed me the cigar, struck the match somewhere behind the bar and passed it to me. I held the flame against the end to carbonize it before putting the cigar to my lips. Then I sucked while holding the match on the end, rotating the cigar against the flame. I blew on the end to stoke it, then on the match to put it out. The result was a well-lit end that would not run on one side. Taking the match from me, the bartender nodded and said, "Enjoy your cigar, sir." Now the sumptuous incense hung in a blue cloud above us.

"Wow," said the man next to me, "that was quite the ceremony. I enjoyed that!"

"I'm sorry, I didn't mean to make it seem theatrical or ceremonious."

"No, it wasn't like that at all. Both you and the bartender were natural, smooth; I didn't get the impression it was contrived if that's what you meant."

"I'm glad. But in a way you're right. It does have something ceremonial to it, but nothing like the Japanese Tea Ceremony, it's more like a tacit etiquette among cigar smokers, like, for example, leaving the tail of the ash as long as possible on the end or never stubbing out a cigar and instead letting it go out by itself in the ashtray. Here in Cuba I'm enjoying smoking where I please."

"Interesting. Where you from? I can't quite place your American accent."

"Yours is easy. You from New Jersey?"

"Nooo, how did you possibly guess?"

"I know. But mine is a long story. I'm from Chicago."

"You sound like you're American, but you certainly don't sound from Chicaga..."

"OK, OK. I'm also from here." I explained the background. "But lived in many places. I've been an expatriate most of my life, so I guess all that molded my accent."

"If you don't mind my asking, how come, don't you like living in the States?"

"Don't get me wrong. I love the U.S. and all it stands for. But you know, I just never bought into that suburban lifestyle so common there. I never liked the sterility of it."

"What do you mean?"

"Well, it's complicated. But you know, like so many places look the same, without their own character. A typical main street has all the familiar McDonalds, Arby's, Wendy's, Taco Bell, etc. The little ma 'n' pa shops are gone; nobody walks, they drive everywhere. The downtowns are empty after five. Neighborhoods aren't really neighborhoods. I mean they're kind of facsimiles of neighborhoods."

"So what do you call a real neighborhood then?"

"Well, to me a real neighborhood is one that everyone in it needs each other."

"Sorry, I don't follow."

"OK, I'll give you the example of where I lived for 12 years, Japan. Japanese cities are really hundreds of self-sufficient neighborhoods. I mean everything you need to live is within walking distance—your fishmonger, your dry-cleaner, your furniture shop, shoe shop, gas station, appliance store, restaurant, pharmacy, bank, everything. What does this mean in sociological terms? Everyone has a vested interest in everyone because everyone depends on everyone. What happens? Everybody knows you and cares for your well-being. Why? Not because they're altruistic, but because they need you and your business. Because of interdependency. The result is you walk home from work and you're greeted all the way home. This type of neighborhood creates personal accountability, a sense of belonging that you don't want to upset. So everyone tends to toe the line of decency. If your kid is misbehaving or troublemaking, you'll hear about it. The 'hood even helps you raise your kid. What's Japan's crime rate? Nothing compared to the States. Now, what happens in much of the States? You live in a neighborhood that is just for residences. If you know your neighbors it's because you've gone out of your way to know them, not because you really needed to. Then you get in your car and you drive 20 miles away to your nearest Walmart or Costco, where about 500,000 people from all different neighborhoods go shop. Nobody knows anybody or has a vested interest in anybody. Anonymity rules. This social setup encourages a sense of estrangement. Look, I'm no sociologist or anything and maybe I'm being simplistic, but have you ever wondered how come in the States there are these mass shootings so often, Columbine and all that? I can't help but think that besides not playing with all their marbles, the common denominator shared by all those shooters is that they all felt alienated from society. What do you think?"

"I think you got something there. And that was a good explanation of a real neighborhood; I see what you mean perfectly. I live in a neighborhood like you described and you're right, most people live in their own little worlds and if they know each other it's because they faked they needed some sugar."

"I'm sure I was oversimplifying and things like that are never that simple, but I'm sure it has something to do with it."

"No, no. What you were talking about were things at the macro level, so they must have some collective influence. Good talking to you. I'm Ben by the way."

I shook his hand and introduced myself.

"So what do you think about Cuba after all these years?"

"Man, don't get me started..." Just then a woman came up and stood a little behind us as if she wanted to order something and we stood a little aside. I asked her if she needed anything from the bartender and she asked for a daiquirí so I ordered one for her and we struck up a conversation. She was a nurse from Vancouver and it was her first time in Cuba. Then Ben, who as it turned out was a marketing specialist, asked her the same question he'd asked me: "What do you think about Cuba?"

"Oh, it's wonderful. I've had such a great time and the people are so nice. And you know, you get a sense of the pride and self-respect that the Revolution has given the people. I mean before there was so much inequality and lack of education and this place was like a playground for Americans."

I said, "You're right about many of those things—sorry, what's your name?"

"Oh, I'm Karen." We introduced ourselves.

"And...," said Ben, looking at me.

"First," you have to remember that the people they allow to work in the tourist industry are hand-picked for their unwavering loyalty to the regime. Right now I'm staying with a nice old couple who have that

143

same sense of pride and self-respect that the Revolution has given them, as you say. Still, there are many good things in this society. For example, I haven't seen any homeless people and everybody seems to get by one way or the other and the people are well educated and have universal health care."

"Now tell us what you really think, Gabe," interjected Ben.

I smiled and began, "Well, Karen, the fact is that this is a totalitarian state..." Karen listened to my argument, now well known to the reader. Then she started on her own: "I hear you, but the U.S. is no angel either and maybe Cuba has to do what it does to stay alive surrounded by American pressure. You know, the embargo, the threat of invasion, the assassination attempts on Castro. So if you think about it, maybe a totalitarian state is the only thing they can do against the constant threats."

"Maybe, but why then does it look and act like every other communist totalitarian state that's *not* been under constant threat from the U.S.? Like China or North Korea. I tend to think the reason is more cynical."

"And what's that?" she asked.

"How about that Fidel Castro is and always has been a megalomaniac and the only way to ensure that he maintained power was to turn to communism and the Soviet Union and install a totalitarian state to hold on to power."

"Why do you say he's a megalomaniac?"

"Because many things about him point to the classic cult of personality so common in totalitarian dictators. Stalin, Mao, Hitler, Mussolini, Saddam Hussein, or Chávez in Venezuela. First, there's no question that Fidel has a big charismatic personality that fills any room he enters. But what I'm talking about goes way over the top. It's the attempt to replace God or imbue a leader with almost god-like qualities to justify remaining in power forever. The message, using total control of mass media, is that 'without me the transformation to a better future can't happen.'" She looked at me skeptically.

"God-like qualities? Come on," said Karen.

"She ain't buyin' it. You better try harder," Ben said, reading her look.

"OK, Karen. Remember the five-hour speeches he used to do?

They'd collect about a million people from the countryside and bus
them to the Plaza de la Revolución so that he'd have a huge audience
and they'd be forced to listen to him in the hot sun for five hours, sometimes more. Now, I ask you, who in the world could possibly be so fas-
cinating that you could listen to him for five hours? Who in the world
would be so presumptuous as to believe he's so interesting that people
would enjoy listening to him for five straight hours? Only a megalomaniac. But he's a very savvy one. Unlike many dictators with the personality cult, he keeps a low profile. There's no monuments to either
Fidel or his brother around. Have you noticed? Only of the dead heroes
like Che and Camilo Cienfuegos. The Castros keep an austere and
modest profile that is in line with the ideology. After all with the people
so poor, it would be incongruous to display wealth. But on the inside,
you can be sure the Castros rule with an iron fist, they take no advice
and Fidel is the alpha and omega of power."

"Whoa! Don't hold nothin' back, dude!"

"Careful," I whispered, feigning wariness, "they might be listening."

"OK, that's pretty convincing. The most interesting person I ever
heard give a speech I couldn't listen to for much more than an hour.
And you're right. That is pretty presumptuous to think that you could
be so interesting."

"Hell, I think Gabe here is pretty interesting," said Ben, "and I
couldn't stand listening to him for more than thirty minutes! That could
be my attention span though, don't take it personally."

"I don't, Ben. Thanks."

"Say how is it you know so much about this place?" asked Karen,
"You seem to know so much about it and your arguments..."

"I'm old. I'm supposed to argue well and yes, I was born here a
long time ago and I've heard all the arguments. So don't be impressed.
What I just told you is old hat."

"Hey," said Ben, "Let's go over there and take a picture with Papa
Hemingway."

"OK, but we'd better get another round for the effect," I said. So
we ordered another and went over to the statue, draping our arms over
the old drinker as a waiter shot us with Ben's iPhone. So much for my
disdain for tourists. We decided to hang out with Papa for a while.

Behind him on the wall was a famous photo I'd seen before: Castro after presenting Hemingway with a prize for some fishing tournament in May of 1960, one of the only photos I've ever seen of Fidel actually listening to someone. Karen asked, "Why did Hemingway love this place so much?"

"Well, he liked the fishing and all that, but I think it was kind of a good match for him. Hemingway, unlike a lot of rich people, wasn't standoffish or pretentious. He really liked being among everyday people and conversing with them. Cubans are and have always been charming and great conversationalists. In the old days, this was just a nice neighborhood bar, not this posh tourist thing they've turned it into. You can see that from these pictures." We looked at other pictures of Papa on the wall and you could see clearly that it was a decent but plain establishment. "You see," I continued, "just a clean well-lighted place, that's all."

"Hey, I remember reading that story," said Ben. "It was about dignity."

"Right, Ben, dignity and correctness, the kinds of things that come from a long history and sophistication. Cuba was the first and last colony of the Spanish and its geographic position allowed it to have more international exchange than any other colony. Hemingway liked this society because of its sophistication, but it was unaffected sophistication, one with dignity and correctness. You might say it had a certain symmetry he enjoyed."

"You a professor or something?" she asked, "You sure talk like one."

"She's hooked me, Ben! Fished me out of the sea. Yes, Karen, you pegged me, a professor. Look, my friends, I have to bid adieu. I got a plane to catch tomorrow." We exchanged e-mail addresses, hugged in the sentimentality of drink and I left.

Stepping outside, the sun was gone and the night was back. I felt a drizzle and it was cooler. Nice for a walk in Old Havana. I turned right into Calle Obispo, still puffing on the cigar. I ignored the odd passerby who offered information, a good time, cigars, women, or music and strode past the bars and cafes, whose most alluring advertisement was the live music coming from within. Coming upon a sidewalk café, I decided to have a nightcap and listen to a band playing across the street. I sat down at one of the tables under the awning and ordered a mojito. A couple came along and the man, smoking a small cigar, said smiling in English, "How are djou, my friend?"

"*Muy bien, chico, y tu, qué tal?*"

"Ah, sounds like you're from around here!" He switched to Spanish.

"I am. But left a long time ago." This was my first mistake.

"Why me too. I tried to leave a few years ago, but I got caught and returned. This place is terrible, huh?"

"In many ways, yes. In others, not."

"Hey, you want to converse a while? Man, I got stories to tell. May we join you?"

"Sure. Sit down." The fact that it was a couple led to my letting my guard down and it didn't help that I was already a little stiff. They sat one on each side of me and introduced themselves. The waiter came and they ordered mojitos. He talked a little about how life was so difficult here and how he hoped to leave again some day. I asked him how he'd got caught.

"I landed on the Florida coast on that leaky boat and the U.S. Coast Guard caught us and returned us. Just when I was feeling the freedom they brought me back to this shit. Hey, I see you like cigars," he said chin-pointing at the one I had put in the ashtray.

"Sure I love them."

"Hey, amigo. You know this thing with fake Cuban cigars is a big racket in Havana. They sell the low-grade stuff to the tourists at the high-grade price"

"They do," said the woman, pointing her crossed legs at me and adding, "You look like a cigar becomes you. Like a gentleman!"

"But man, I can get the real stuff for you but not at the price for the tourist, but the price for the people. Do you want to try one? They sell them right here at this café."

"Sure," I said, "But..." He got up and came back a minute later with 25 small cigars in a round bundle. He took one and gave it to me. It lit up like a cigarette.

"What do you think? Nice, huh?"

"It's OK."

"I got this at a special price because I know the owner and it's yours for 20 CUC. Man, I just did you a deal you won't regret."

"You mean you already paid for this bundle?" He nodded. "That's too bad because I didn't ask you to get it for me."

"But you have to pay us!" protested the woman.

"Really? Why is that?"

"Because what he just paid and look at you, you're rich and we are poor!"

"Lady, I worked hard for everything I have and I didn't cheat anyone to get it, which is what you're trying to do to me." I looked at the man to my left and he had closed his eyes and was rubbing his forehead with his fingers. "How much did you pay for this? Shall I ask the waiter?"

"Please don't ask the waiter, man," he said, alarm in his voice.

"You're not fair!" cried the woman, now writhing in her seat, "You're so lucky. Americans! Life is so hard for us. And now we're stuck with this bill!"

"Life is hard? Well, why don't you rebel instead of swindle? And you," turning to the man, "if you landed on the coast of Florida, that means you were on U.S. soil and they couldn't have sent you back. By law they had to take you in. You were never on any boat to Florida. And besides, these are worthless cigars and you know it." I turned to the woman. She was crying on her way to hysterics. I looked at the man, his head down, rubbing his forehead.

"Oh, Jesus. Look, I'll do this for you, I'll buy your mojitos, but the cigars are yours." I stood, took out enough for the drinks, put it on the table and walked away back toward Parque Central. "How could I have been so stupid? How so stupid, at my age?" I kept berating myself all the way to Casa Sandra.

DAY TEN

Upon awakening, I realized I had just enough cash left to make it home—with no room for niceties. I bid a heartfelt goodbye to Sandra and Silvio and went off to the airport with Vladimir, the taxi driver who'd brought me.

"Vladimir, you were right about Sandra and Silvio," I started, "Die hard communists, but really nice people."

"The best," he said, "but a dying breed."

"Do you think if the Castros die, Cuba will open up? It will all go away?"

"Why should it? They'll hand pick a successor on their deathbed. Maybe Fidel's oldest son, Fidelito. But nobody knows much about him or the other sons. Or El Caballo (The Horse, Fidel's nickname) will pick someone from the politburo of the National Assembly, maybe Juan Lazo the current president. But whoever it is, the Castros will be sure that the same old policies will be kept by the new man."

"Ok, so that means rebellion is the only avenue of change. Why don't the people rebel? Why haven't they rebelled in over fifty years?"

"I've thought about that many times and come to the conclusion that there's lots of reasons, but it's mainly because the CDR nip the opposition at the grassroots level. This group gets to any budding organization before it even has time to organize. It has 200,000 neighborhood stations and millions of members. It is likely the single most important government group responsible for the domestic security of Cuba. Every square block in Cuba has its own committee. They do much civil and socially oriented work such as cleanup crews, street repair, recycling efforts, energy conservation, but in reality their community aid work is as much a front and facilitator for its central function: to watch the activities of the citizens of every block in Cuba and report "irregularities," in other words, to protect Cuba (also known as the regime) from Cubans."

"Yes, some organization. What about Las Damas de Blanco (the Ladies in White, an opposition group composed of wives of political prisoners)? How did they get through the CDR and are allowed to protest openly."

"They protest, but not without harrassment. And to answer your question, the fact that they are women helps them. If they were men they'd never have gotten off the ground. They are not seen as much of a threat and to abuse or mistreat women physically is a real taboo in Cuban society. So the regime has no choice but to tolerate them—as long as they don't start getting a big following, which they haven't yet."

"And there's the control of education and the media," I added. "You know, talking to Silvio is like talking to some religious fanatic, but instead of bringing up God in every other sentence he brings up the Castros."

"You're right. Of course, you know that the government is officially atheist. But in fact, they are the new religion."

"Well said, Vladimir. But you know part of it is also that the regime does provide for the people in some very basic needs; education, health and a roof over your head: there are no homeless here, and so that tends to quiet complaints and to disarm the people morally regarding rebellion."

"Sure it disarms them. But you know, most people don't really have much ambition. Most are content to live life from day to day. And those are the people most content with this government. But if you have ambition and you have a dream you'd tend to hate this system because it isn't made for people with new ideas or ways, it's made for perpetuating itself at the expense of people's dreams."

It didn't escape me that I was conversing with a taxi driver about some rather abstract ideas not normally associated with the intellectual capacity of taxi drivers. The idiosyncrasies of Cuba awed me. I said, "Look what happened to the professionals in the 60's, they all went to Miami. Fidel suddenly woke up one day and he had practically no one left around who knew how to run the country. So he ended the flights to Miami and had to have a bunch of East Bloc professionals come and do the job."

"That's right. Smart people don't like this crap. They know too much and know how to think. It's always a problem for the regime.

They educate people to a certain level, then these are the people that most often become their enemies—unless they fall prey to pretending their way through life. But let me ask you, what were the good things you saw here?"

"Well, no homelessness; everyone seems to manage at a basic level; everyone I met has been at least decently educated; the people have social glue, a sense of community; music, the arts, sports are well supported; the musicians are well cared for; I didn't see any racial or class discrimination; the people seem to have the same cheerful spirit they always had. Oh and I forgot: you have one freedom here lost now to most of the world."

"What's that?"

"The freedom to smoke wherever you want. So there are many good things."

"Yes, there are good things. And like you said, it disarms the people and it has a lot to do with why they don't rebel—for most it may not be worth the risk of dying."

"What about the risk of dying on your way to Miami in a rickety boat in one of the most shark-infested straits in the world?"

"I said, for most; there are plenty of desperate enough people; people who have been marginalized by the regime or people who have dreams. But hell, that's another way they stay in power—many malcontents leave instead of rebel. It's kind of like a pressure release valve. Here we are."

He helped me with my bag and shook my hand as with the other he gave me his calling card. "I hope to see you again someday. Look me up next time you're in Cuba."

"You are the smartest taxi driver I ever met. Of course, I'll look you up! By the way, what were you before you became a chauffeur?"

"I was a professor. And you?"

"A professor." He laughed. I laughed. He got in and drove away.

"What an incredible taxi driver!" I said to myself. "Now that was refreshing, considering the average cabbie in New York is a Third World sociopath." I shrugged and went inside.

The tall aristocratic woman in front of me at the check-in line turned and looked at me as she heard me approach. Our eyes met and I said hello.

"Did you like your stay in Cuba?" I asked.

"Of course, did you?"

"Yes and no. I was generally disappointed in what has become of my country. It could be a lot better, don't you think?"

Frowning slightly, her eyes darted a bit. "You're not from here? I can't quite place your accent."

"I left a long time ago and lived many places. The old accent comes out only when I drink. Sounds like you're Argentine. But you didn't answer my question."

Her eyes beckoned mine to look down at her hands folded under the open passport that had DIPLOMAT backgrounded on both pages. When I looked up at her eyes again, she was already looking at mine and whispered, "I'm sorry," with genuine tone and look.

"I understand," I whispered back. She turned toward the counter and the conversation ended. "I should have been more tactful," I said to myself. "Too brash. I guess didn't live in America for 25 years for nothing."

Standing behind that lovely Argentine, I thought of the United States, the nemesis, in its own evolution as the greatest socio-economic experiment in history, as one of the world's oldest democracies, uniting all the cultures of the world under its flag. It then struck me that I should not only be sad about Cuba; I should also be sad about America. My explanation to Ben about why I didn't live in the States whirled through my mind. Neighborhoods created by zoning laws to contain only residences, the destruction of the ma 'n' pa shops, the advent of the malls and the Walmarts and the Costcos. The sterilization of America. The alienation, the anonymity of life. Americans have allowed the creation of communities that do little for them and much for big business. They have allowed a misled capitalist system to determine the breakneck pace of life that even back in the 70's Alvin Toffler warned us about in *Future Shock*. Far from giving us more free "quality" time, modern life and especially the Internet have created the demand for more accomplishment in less time. The marketing machine seduced us by pulling the strings of marionettes named Lust, Vanity, Sloth, Envy, Greed, and most of all the one called Fear, the hidden levers in any given advertisement. They've let illusions and obsessions created by "The Machine" run their life. I say "Americans have allowed this"

152

because in a capitalist democracy who else can you blame but the people? Our fault lies in our disdain for the great power we have in not only to vote but also to vote with our money.

We've let capitalism be centralized (in the hands of a few and in multinationals) and have allowed it to centralize our lives. The deterioration of the middle class and its buying power has forced both adults in the nuclear family to work when in the past only one was needed. To sustain the same quality of life, Americans were encouraged by the marketers to use credit cards to compensate for their withered buying power. This last thought reminded me of the day back in the 1970's when I saw my father cutting his credit cards to pieces in order to decide to live within his means—a lesson I never forgot, for I have never been in debt and have never "owned" a credit card. "What are you doing, Pops?" I asked him as he cut away.

"If you *need* to use credit cards, you can't afford them," he answered in a resigned voice.

Bill Clinton and many congressmen, under pressure from Wall Street and bank lobbies, pushed for the repeal of the Glass-Steagall Act of 1933, which regulated lending practices, separated commercial banks from Wall Street and forbid banks from underwriting securities and selling insurance. The deregulation and the ensuing lending free-for-all set the stage for what became the greatest finanacial crisis since the Great Depression. Then George Bush said one day, "We want everybody in America to own their own home. That's what we want." The resulting permissive lending environment led to the debacle that's all too familiar. All this happened while the entire nation was distracted by the adrenalin of their credit-driven buying spree, not to mention the 1000 channels of crap.

Americans climbed the bandwagon with all the mindlessness of the herd. They went ahead and voted with their money, or rather, money they didn't have. This they did with an aplomb and naiveté never before witnessed in the history of the nation: Within a few years Americans were buying twice the amount of clothing per year as they had bought when they hadn't literally bought into debt as a way of life. People on a massive scale were now buying for vanity rather than need. Buy a home and use the home itself as the collateral for the loan! Never mind the happenstance of the worst scenario, full speed ahead! Never mind that if the location is first and foremost in investing in real estate, why in the world would you buy a home in a place where you have *to drive miles* to get anything you want? Why would you place a business miles from your clients? That set up was wonderful for the land developer: The land parceled all in one large area, he saved much in legal, transportation, labor, tax and construction costs. Detroit and Big Oil had a ball since cars and the gas to run them became indispensable. On paper, it all looked so neat. Everything in its place divided by function. How modern! Good for the big time investor and politician, but bad for the people that live there, for the environment and society.

The seduction of marketing drove too many Americans (more than half of Americans live in suburbs), individualists at heart, towards the lawn, the picket fence, and the remote little castle of one's own little world. What made it possible was that the marketers knew an old lesson: The middle class has always tried to imitate nobility or the rich. It is perfectly reasonable, if one is rich, to live separated from society in some luxurious and remote castle (the Hearst Castle popped to mind). One has servants and resources enough so that there is no inconvenience. But that set up makes little sense for the middle class with their limited income and the onerous expense of buying, insuring, and maintaining cars. A European friend once observed that America's towns and cities seemed to him designed for the convenience and comfort of cars, not people. "Everything is so big and everything is far away in America," he said. "American cities and towns are not for pedestrians; they lack humanity."

I thought of my friend, whom I will call Harold, and his neighborhood in a posh Miami suburb. Huge mansions everywhere, each housing a small family; vast, ever thirsty, ever trimmed lawns; nothing is in walking distance; save for the occasional jogger or dog walker there are no pedestrians; the closest business is a gas station 2 miles away and across the street from it there's a Seven Eleven; the Costco that Harold is a member of, and where he gets practically everything, is 30 minutes away by car. He and his wife know their immediate neighbors only as people they wave to when they happen to also enter or leave their house. His three sons are bored and find the suburb boring although they have everything in the world to keep them entertained: smartphones, a TV in each bedroom with a thousand channels, a personal car, video games, a PC, and all the toys in the modern world for adolescents. Yet they suffer from ennui. Like their parents, they interact with no one in the neighborhood. I'm reminded of one of Jon Krakaouer's quotes from *Into the Wild*: "Happiness is only real when shared."[1] But so many in America have bought into creating and living in the islands of solitude that are their homes in the suburbs.

In most ways, capitalism trounces communism, but it is far from perfect, and it has one overriding flaw: when it comes to the bottom line, it has no conscience. As the first Prime Minister of India, Jawaharlal Nehru, once said, "The forces in a capitalist society, if left unchecked tend to make the rich richer and the poor poorer." The evidence and wisdom of this aphorism mount as we advance into the 21st century.

But capitalism doesn't have to be scrapped, it simply has to return, at least to a significant extent, to its roots, the state it was in during the grand majority of its existence before the advent of today's globalization.

Because of a growing awareness by citizens of many places around the world that the laissez-faire model of capitalism is essentially flawed, many communities are attempting to bring it back to its founding, more human roots, a movement called Community Capitalism. Towns like Prien am Chiemsee, Bavaria, and Kalamazoo, Michigan, Ithaca in New York State, Bristol in South West England, and the small countries of Bhutan and Nepal in South Asia have established local capitalism that emphasizes the well-being and sustainability of each community, not just of the now proverbial 1 percent.[2] Most to the point, the Kingdom of Bhutan, whose King Jigme Singye, realizing that the Gross National Product Index is really an index to the economic well-being of the 1 percent, supplanted the international standard of growth with what he called the Gross National Happiness Index for his own country. When I first read about this back in 2000 while I was in Japan, it resonated with common sense, for in the end, what are we here for if not for the pursuit of happiness, *everyone's* happiness?

Then I thought of where I live in Costa Rica, in Puerto Jiménez, a small town of about 8,000 that rests in the Osa Peninsula by the Golfo Dulce (literally, The Sweet Gulf, but the actual meaning is the Fresh Water Gulf, "sweet" water means fresh water in Spanish) on the southern Pacific coast. It's a place so imbued with humanity that women suckle their babes in public and no one raises an eyebrow. People walk or ride bikes everywhere, helping them stay healthy and slim. I walk down the main street and practically everyone that passes me says hello or calls out one of the names the town has adopted for me, "Don Gabriel" or "El Profe" (The Professor). I am respected and the people have accepted me as one of their own probably because I have respected and treated them well. I have a strong feeling of belonging and caring for this town that has little crime, little stress, and enormous natural beauty—macaws, monkeys and iguanas in the trees and dolphins, whales and turtles in the gulf. I bought, without financing, a modest and decent house with the nearest supermarket, bank, hardware store,

From Puerto Jiménez, a view of El Golfo Dulce. Across the gulf is the town of Golfito, where Che Guevara spent some days in 1953 on his way north to eventually meet Fidel Castro in Mexico. It was in Golfito that he visited the "dominions of the United Fruit Company," perhaps the quintessence of the exploitative multinational.

shoe repair, gas station, restaurant and bakery all within 300 meters. I walk or ride my bicycle everywhere and don't need a car for most needs. Time does not hound but accompanies me. My life is simple and happily shared with those around me. I have people with whom I can see the reflection of my existence as if I were in front of a sentient mirror and said, "Isn't that Golfo Dulce beautiful?" And the mirror would say, "Yes, I never get tired of looking at it either." A city boy all my life, it surprised me when I realized that this was the first place I'd ever lived in that did not disquiet my spirit.

I also thought of Cuba and how it could all have been better if *they* had just let the people be themselves instead of trying to turn them into *their* own image and likeness, a god-like attribute no one should endure. Guevara never saw that the existentially tortured "sick, spiteful, unattractive man" in *Notes from Underground* was sounding the depths of his humanity: irrational, compelled, and afraid. Hardly the stuff on which to build Utopia. The "utopia" they forced on the people caused them to depend on each other. Therefore, Cubans have the strong sense of community lacking in America. For them, time is timeless, free and irrelevant. Time has not been made to equal money and it is what it was meant to be: the dimension in which the rhythm of everything in the other three dimensions moves. They have also been spared the insanity of today's consumerism, its obsessions and illusions. It is a worthy and ironic observation that a socio-economic system based on the acceptance of human nature (capitalism) has diminished the "humanity" of its society, while a system that has rejected human nature (communism) has engendered humanity in its own. In many ways, Cuban society *is* more humane—unless you don't toe the line. But if you do, then the regime, for the most part, manages to provide the most elementary physical needs: housing, health care, food rations, and the mental one, education. In Havana, I saw a generalized but just bearable poverty, not the kind all too abundant in many Latin countries and even in America—extreme poverty. The kind where you don't have shelter and must sift through garbage to survive.

Therefore, a debate may arise pitting the value of human rights, democracy and capitalism against the value in providing the minimum for everyone at the expense of their human rights. Although it tortures and beats prisoners, arrests people for mere suspicion and manacles free expression, the regime has some self-imposed limits. While Cuba is a totalitarian state, it is a relatively soft one. It is not North Korea or Stalinist Russia, or Mao's China, regimes that built assembly lines of death, factories whose product was corpses. Instead, the regime's relationship with its people is not unlike that between a traditional master and dog. The master provides shelter (squalid), food (minimal), and training (in what he wants you to think), but demands loyalty, obedience and gratitude. If he doesn't get them, well, the master chains and whips the dog. But people deserve better and there is no need to chain and whip them so that they have a roof over their head. Even dogs deserve better.

The plane circled over Havana before turning south toward Costa Rica. I wondered if I would ever return and if the Castros would be there, still dictating life. Although as always I missed Puerto Jiménez when I left it for long, I felt a hollowness inside me I had not felt since the last time a woman broke my heart. The French have a saying for such occasions: *Partir c'est mourir un peu.* To leave is to die a little. And I felt a part of me die as Havana faded into blue.

Three hours later I landed in San José and the next day a small plane flew me to Jiménez.

EPILOGUE

In the weeks that followed, I kept in touch with Sandra and Silvio through e-mail to coordinate their sending me the birth certificate. A month later I had the certificate in my hands, stamped by both the Costa Rican Embassy and the Cuban Exterior Ministry. I sent Sandra and Silvio some money to cover their costs and more. We kept writing to each other. At that time, Hugo Chávez was constantly in the news because of his battle with cancer and his frequent trips to Cuba for treatment. I wondered how a public figure could be so secretive about the details of his disease when elections were coming soon and the people should be informed so that they would know if they were going to vote for a president or a soon-to-be-corpse. When I was in Havana four months before the election, he had declared himself completely cured (as Silvio had said). In November, he easily won his fourth term as president. But right after the election, they disclosed that Chávez would return to Cuba for another operation. The inauguration was to be held in January and the president-elect was not going to be able to attend. The Venezuelan constitution states that if a president-elect is incapacitated for his inauguration, new elections must be held within 30 days. The constitution was violated and no elections were held until after March 5, 2013—when Vice President Nicolás Maduro announced that Hugo Chávez was dead.

As all this was happening, I was exchanging e-mails with Sandra and Silvio, and although I had promised myself to not challenge them politically with respect to Cuba, I saw nothing wrong with challenging them a little with regard to Venezuela. In one of those messages I wrote that people here in Costa Rica couldn't understand how Chávez, holding the highest office and now up for re-election, was being so secretive about the nature and extent of his cancer. Here was their reply; Sandra wrote:

Epilogue

Dear Gabriel:

The content of your letter with respect to the concealment about Chávez's illness in Venezuela truly surprises us. Just think that when it was decided that he should return to Cuba in order to submit to another operation, Chávez himself talked before the cameras to the people and the rest of the world, explaining all the details, how long it would take, characteristics, etc. From then on after the operation, every other day and sometimes daily, they began to issue reports explaining the state of his health. And so we have been able to follow his progress throughout and thanks to the information provided we know that there were huge crowds in Caracas in front of which on a few occasions Commandant Nicolás Maduro spoke to those multitudes informing the people of everything that was happening and here in Cuba we could see and hear all this perfectly just as in other countries. Therefore, we don't understand where this comes from, we truly don't. In Spain, for example, where they get Cubavision International, everyone is up to date on the news.

Don't you in Costa Rica, as a Latin American country, have access to Telesur? But furthermore, news also comes out on the Internet. One has to wonder if this rumor comes from Costa Rica; I don't know..., you know what the press is like, distorting everything. Why recently El Pais [Spain's largest daily] published a false article with a false photo of a patient in a hospital, claiming it was Chávez and that he was dying. It was proven false in every way to the extent that even the Spanish had to admit it. Incidentally, Rajoy, the president of Spain, was in Chile at that time, and like other heads of state, was able to hear the message sent by Chávez himself about the entire process of recovery he was facing. Now recently a meeting of CELAC [Comisión de Estados Latinoamericanos y del Caribe, Commission of Latin American and Caribbean States, created by Chávez] was held in Chile, which formerly held the organization's presidency, now held by Cuba. During that meeting, an EU meeting was also held and it is for that reason that I tell you Rajoy was there. It is incredible how disinformation and distortion affect the people since already in Costa Rica they say that Chávez's condition is unknown. This is truly UNBELIEVABLE. I wish you could see the people of Venezuela in the streets seeking places where they could hear information; people were interviewed and said that they knew that their President would return because he would withstand it all and that God would accompany him like he always has.

Finally, my brother, we don't know what else to tell you, but we can reiterate that it is totally false that in Venezuela nothing is known about Chávez's illness. This is completely inadmissible. Sooner than later, like Chávez's second said, Chávez will be in Venezuela because, furthermore, he has been kept informed of everything in all aspects.

Please accept as always our greatest affection as we send you a strong hug. (Please write to tell us if you understood all this and please find out about Telesur, which transmits almost daily).

Affectionately,
Sandra and Silvio

This was what I expected from them. Telesur is a satellite and cable news channel owned by several leftist Latin American states. It broadcasts in Costa Rica, although through a cable provider I don't subscribe to. It is a well-known fact that Chávez never revealed what type of cancer he suffered or all he knew about its progress; he only stated that a baseball-sized tumor had been removed from his pelvis in the first operation in 2011. It was not until early 2012, that Wikileaks published internal e-mails (stolen from Stratfor, an Austin-based analytical firm) that revealed that the alternate teams of specialists from Cuba and Russia that treated Chávez were in conflict. The Russian doctors blamed the Cubans for botching Chávez' first cancer surgery and had had to "clean up the Cuban team's mistakes."[1] One e-mail further states that "A reliable source on the medical team has explained that the cancer has spread to the lymph nodes and into the bone marrow up to the spine, i.e., very serious." In other words, metastasis. The people of Venezuela had been disinformed for political reasons into voting for a dead man walking.

Here's my response to Sandra and Silvio:

Hello my dear friends,

Thank you for your explanation. At this end, I have the news from NTN, CNN, BBC, and TVE as well as the local Costa Rican channels. We get Telesur, but it is on another cable network I don't have. I'm also aware of the publication of the false photo of Chávez and the retraction by El País. But to give you an idea of what is not known about the Chávez illness, I'd like to know if you know the answer to the following: What kind of cancer does he have? Has it metastasized (since there have already been four operations)? What are the chances for a complete recovery? What is the prognosis of the doctors for his improvement or otherwise? Why didn't he stay in Venezuela to be operated on since in Venezuela the doctors are as competent as they are anywhere in South America? These are the questions that people want to have answered, especially the opposition, but all we know is that "Chávez is getting better, progressing well, etc." In other words, no details—only optimistic generalities. This is what is meant by "concealment." I know that his party supports him 100 percent, but not everyone and these are the citizens that he must also serve for he is after all their employee as well. The constitution was already violated for his benefit. The law was very clear: If the president-elect is unable to attend the inauguration, the nation has 30 days to organize new elections in which new presidential candidates will compete for the presidency. These are the things that have many people here doubting if in Venezuela what exists is a democracy or simply the dictatorship of the majority. Well, my friends, I leave you here and I hope you continue writing.

A big hug from,
Gabriel

I never heard from them again.

The Great Divide continues. And it will always continue because the young and the poor, having nothing, will without end have nothing to lose with revolution and change, while the old and the rich, having everything, will always have everything to lose by them. In the end, the best we can do is what *all* of us can do: change and revolutionize ourselves for the better and our communities and the world will follow.

At the heart of the Great Divide, however, is not wealth, but how we regard it—as *everything* in the United States and as *nothing* in Cuba. Both are extremes and both, wrong, so wrong that the Great Divide divided *me*. I've ended up an exile from both countries that most shaped me. I'm an exile from Cuba because the regime took everything from my family, including our freedom, and from America because I always sought to live somewhere more human and less sterile, where humanity has not taken a back seat to materialism and "Big Business." One might say I became an exile from Cuba for mainly material reasons and from America, for spiritual ones. I recall an awakening I had one day about what is the bridge between the American and Cuban extremes, an epiphany about a treasure, light and portable, that will yield all that is material and spiritual in the world. In America this wealth, the only one of any value, too often serves materialism; in Cuba it serves the perpetuation of the regime, but at least America dispenses the treasure without strings attached. It happened 10 years after we had left Miami and gone to Chicago...

The old man still taught at the university and still had his nightly talks with Mr. Faycund. Pops, now in his early 60's had never lost his penchant for self-improvement for he was studying for his master's degree in Latin American literature. He had created a considerable library and tended to read it. He was a full participant in American culture, who never missed the weekly *Ed Sullivan Show*, or the *Honeymooners*, the *Carroll Burnett Show*, or the *Danny Kaye Show*, all of whose antics sparked in him uproarious laughter. Indeed, Pops never lost the little boy in himself; he loved to laugh and lose himself in the moment, a habit he would take to his grave. A powerful chess player in his days in Cuba, he rarely could find strong opponents, so he would now spend hours playing over the matches of the grandmasters. "I don't recommend chess, my son; it is a beautiful waste of time," he had told me that day in Havana when he'd taught me how the pieces moved. Of course, I didn't listen and I have been wasting my time beautifully with it ever since.

One day in the summer of 1972, enjoying his vacation by following a Capablanca match in the living room, Pops suddenly looked up from the chessboard and declared, "We're going to buy a Buick and we're going to Miami to break it in!"

Late at night after a leisurely three-day trip, the brand new Buick, motor purring, slid into the parking lot of the Fontainebleau Hotel in Miami Beach. There was a guard house at the end of the driveway that led to the hotel's façade. The guard asked Pops in broken English with a strong Spanish accent, "Guest o visitor?"

"Guest."

"Go guest valet parking on right," and handed him a large square plastic chip labeled GUEST.

Pops took his chip and drove toward the front entrance. Turning off the engine at the portal, he settled back in the seat in thought. "You know, Consuelo, I think I know that man."

"The guard?"

"*Sí, chica.* Unless I'm wrong.... Let's see." He gave the keys to the bellhop that had come to the window and we stepped out of the car and followed the old man who walked ahead, his neck craned, hawk-eyeing the guardhouse. As we approached, something made the guard, a tall corpulent man of sixty-some, turn frowning our way. Drawing nearer, my father flung out his arms, then the guard's face cleared, but with a hint of shame.

"*Coño,* Joselito! What the devil are you doing here?"

"Cundo! Damn it, what a pleasure! How long has it been? *Chico!*"

Pops closed his arms to hug him and the two slapped each other on the back. They let go and Pops turned to us and said, "Consuelo, I was right; it's Josélito Infante! Can you believe it?"

"*Que tal,* Josélito! What pleasure!" and they hugged. "Do you remember the boys, Facundito and Gabriel?"

My father, Facundo, when young, circa 1933. Castro took everything away from him except what was of greatest value. When he stood naked before the world, he was prepared.

"Boys? I wouldn't have recognized them; why they're a pair of grown men!" He extended his big hand and we shook it in greeting.

"But Joselito, what a surprise!" said the old man. "The last time we saw each other was your daughter's debutante party. How long ago, 11, 12 years, remember? Another cloud crossed Joselito's face. Although I was only seven, I still recalled that golden afternoon in Havana Harbor aboard Joselito Infante's luxury yacht.

"*Sí, chico,* but I'm afraid there'll no longer be afternoons like that one. His eyes welled, tears overflowed the lids and his lower lip trembled in spite of a great struggle for self-control. Then something was unleashed inside and he wept, shoulders heaving.

"*Ay*, Joselito," father said, again hugging him. "It kills me to see you like this. Don't worry, my friend, everything will turn out well."

"No, Cundo. They took everything from us ... and now.... I'm just a useless old man. You can see it. I can't speak English and with no profession... The old man had left me with everything and I... You know very well, Cundo."

Thus, they remained in the gloom: a big man crying in the arms of one smaller, who tried to console him. After the sobs relented, in spite of his objections, father put $100 in his shirt pocket. He invited him to dinner the next day and, taking turns hugging him, we each said goodnight.

It wasn't then that I realized what I had witnessed. I knew what had happened in the concrete sense, but it was not until much later, after I had entered university that autumn, that I came to understand what had happened in the abstract. I remember it was during a class on the Holocaust and the Jews that my eyes opened. And from then on I began, like never before in my life I began, just like my dear old man, I began to study.

Although he doesn't know me and I am just one of the countless pawns he moved about the chessboard in his quest for power, the irony is I have to thank Fidel Castro. I am an old man looking back on his life and trying to make some sense of it all. I know I must stand in humility before the force of history and the great wind that blew through that island of my youth and swept away everything I was meant to be. A hard question we all should ask ourselves is: What is left to me if I stand naked and alone before the world? Now I know that if Fidel Castro had not had his Revolution, I would have been a richer, yet far poorer man.

Notes

Prologue

1. Ribero Caro, *Cuba: The Unnecessary Revolution.*
2. Bosch, *The American Experience: Fidel Castro.*
3. Thomas, *Cuba or The Pursuit of Freedom,* p. 919.
4. *Ibid.,* pp. 919–920.
5. *Ibid.,* p. 921.
6. Bosch, *The American Experience: Fidel Castro.*
7. *Ibid.*
8. Geyer, *The Unexpected Lives of Fidel Castro.*
9. Wikipedia, The Free Encyclopedia, *Blanqueamiento.*

Day Two

1. Anderson, *Che Guevara,* p. 237.
2. Thomas, *Cuba,* p. 1470.
3. *Ibid.,* p. 1471.
4. *Ibid.,* p. 1470.
5. *Ibid.,* p. 1470.
6. Laretsky, *Ernesto Che Guevara,* p. 5.
7. Anderson, *Che Guevara,* pp. 37–38.
8. Taibo, *Guevara,* p. 31.
9. Thomas, *Cuba,* p. 1470.
10. Burns and Charlip, *Latin America,* p. 106.
11. Torres Rivera, "The Coups d'Etat in Latin America" 2010.
12. Thomas, *Cuba,* p. 738.

Day Three

1. Rosenfleder, *U.S. Interventions in Latin America.*
2. Kirkpatrick, *Dictatorships and Double Standards.*
3. SPJ Code of Ethics, www.spj.org.

Day Five

1. Kirk, *José Martí,* p. 278.

Day Six

1. Muller, *Cuba's Secret Side.*

2. Reuters, *"Castro Comments."*
3. Ager and Yearsley, *Masters of Money.*

Day Ten

1. Penn & Krakauer, *Into the Wild.*
2. Borrel, *Invisible (R)evolutions.*

Epilogue

1. Wyss, "WikiLeaks: Doctors of Venezuela's Hugo Chávez."

BIBLIOGRAPHY

Ager, Sarah, and Will Yearsley, *Masters of Money: The World According to Marx* (documentary). BBC, 2012.

Anderson, Jon Lee. *Che Guevara: A Revolutionary Life*. New York: Grove Press, 1997.

Borrel, Philippe. *Invisible Revolutions* (documentary). Cinétévé, 2014.

Bosch, Adriana. *The American Experience: Fidel Castro* (PBS). Boston: WGBH Educational Foundation, 2005.

Burns, E. Bradford, and Julie A. Charlip. *Latin America: An Interpretative History*. Upper Saddle River, New Jersey: Pearson Education, 2007.

Geyer, Georgie Anne "The Unexpected Lives of Fidel Castro: Fidel Castro: I don't care what happens to Cuba after I'm dead." www.freerepublic.com, 2006.

Kirk, John M. *José Martí: Mentor of the Cuban Nation*. Tampa: University Presses of Florida, 1977

Kirkpatrick, Jeane. "Dictatorships and Double Standards," *Commentary Magazine*, Volume 68, No. 5, November 1979.

Laretsky, Iosif. *Ernesto Che Guevara*. Moscow, 1976.

Muller, Karin, *Cuba's Secret Side* (documentary). Firelight Productions, 2013.

Penn, Sean, and Jon Krakauer. *Into the Wild* (screenplay based on Krakauer book). Paramount Pictures, 2007.

Reuters. "Castro Comments on Cuban Prostitution" CNN, May 1, 2001 (http://latinamericanstudies.org/cuba/castro-prostitution.htm).

Ribero Caro, Adolfo. "Cuba: The Unnecessary Revolution," www. neoliberalismo.com.

Rosenfleder, Mark. "U.S. Interventions in Latin America," www.zompist.com, 1996.

Society of Professional Journalists. SPJ Code of Ethics, www.spj.org.

Taibo, Paco Ignacio, II. *Guevara, Also Known as Che*, 2d ed. New York: St. Martin's Griffin, 1999.

Thomas, Hugh. *Cuba or The Pursuit of Freedom*. New York: Da Capo Press, 1998.

Torres Rivera, Alejandro. "The Coups d'Etat in Latin America and the Dangers Facing Venezuela." Essay, 2010, from website (http://venezuelanalysis.com).

Wikipedia, The Free Encyclopedia. www.wikipedia.org.

Wyss, Jim. "WikiLeaks: Doctors of Venezuela's Hugo Chávez Disagree over His Health." *Miami Herald*, February 2012.

INDEX

Index